M000092832

THE GHOST OF HENRY PUTT AND OTHER FIREHOUSE TALES

THE GHOST OF HENRY PUTT AND OTHER FIREHOUSE TALES

RICH GRIMM

JONES MEDIA PUBLISHING

The Ghost of Henry Putt and Other Firehouse Tales Copyright © 2020 by Rich Grimm.

All rights reserved. No part of this publication may be reproduced, distributed, or transmitted in any form or by any means, including photocopying, recording, or other electronic or mechanical methods, without the prior written permission of the author, except in the case of brief quotations embodied in critical reviews and certain other noncommercial uses permitted by copyright law.

Jones Media Publishing
10645 N. Tatum Blvd. Ste. 200-166
Phoenix, AZ 85028
www.JonesMediaPublishing.com

Disclaimer:

Although this publication is designed to provide accurate information in regard to the subject matter covered, the publisher and the author assume no responsibility for errors, inaccuracies, omissions, or any other inconsistencies herein.

Printed in the United States of America

ISBN: 978-1-948382-11-3 paperback
JMP2020.4

he rig. We had a couple of pretty good ripping fires
as just Q Ball, the paid firefighter, and a few long-
mply faced teenagers that put out the fire. We were
do everything except drive the equipment. You had
teen for that due to insurance restrictions. (And of
 didn't call the chief Q Ball to his face!)

would host weekly training on pumping, hose lays,
rs. We would go over fire attack and do breathing
drills with covered, blacked out breathing apparatus
he station to find the rescue dummy. He showed a
ence with not only the younger guys but the older,
uys, who volunteered their time but couldn't make
training days. We would also go to the county fire
 the regional airport a few times per year. We did in
-aid training with the Red Cross and even learned a
 technique called CPR!

nately, my dad had a terrible work accident in
vas on a phone pole about fifteen feet up when he
fell. He never remembered much about it. He was
roken up and probably should have died. He was
pital for weeks. When he got out of the hospital,
do rehab and slowly got back to somewhat normal.
 company gave him an office job, and that really
vind out of his sails. He missed being outside and
m of climbing poles. It was also difficult, because
vays talked about fighting fires together, and by the
ed the department, he was limited to helping pick
 directing traffic. He couldn't get very involved in
ack, but he still loved being a part of it all.

red light, shaped like a bubble gum machine, on the roof and a siren wailing away under the hood. He always kept his turnout gear in the trunk. I would be with him once in a while out running errands when a call would come in. The fire station sat on the highest part of the town, with a huge air-raid-type siren that would go off if there was a fire call. It also had a tall antenna that had a giant red light that would rotate when the siren went off to alert all of the town's volunteers.

I would love it when we went to calls together. I got to see all sorts of crazy things as a little kid. Car crashes, house fires, grass fires, and we even had a helicopter crash-land just down the street from our house when I was six or seven.

So, this was my stand. To get my mom to say yes to being able to always go with my dad, anytime, day or night.

"Come on mom, I've already been with dad on some calls, and you know I just stay in the car. I *promise* you I won't leave the car and do whatever dad tells me to do. I promise!"

My mom just sat there, listening, taking very long drags on her Old Gold cigarettes, and sipping her coffee.

After about a half an hour of my begging and pleading, she looked over at my dad. Now, my mom had one of those glares that could melt the iceberg that sunk the Titanic. She shot a look at my six-foot-one, 240-pound, ex-football playing father with laser beams coming out of her eyes.

"OK, he can go with you. But if anything happens to him, I will kill you, *understood*?"

Wait, what! Did my mom just agree to let me ride along with my dad anytime? I think hell just froze over.

My dad assured her that everything will be fine. I cleaned up the table and did the dishes, scraping half eaten fishy hockey pucks into the trash can. I couldn't believe it! My dad just gave me a quick glance and a wink.

All was good in my world.

My mom and dad adopted me when I was a baby. They had been waiting a long time for me to arrive, so they were even more protective than the average parents. Our little town was typical Americana. We had great neighbors, and everyone knew each other. Fridays were for high school football; Saturday was for the Ohio State Buckeyes and Sundays were for church. We lived on the state line of Ohio and Pennsylvania. Dad worked for the phone company, good ole Ma Bell, or simply Bell. He climbed poles and installed just about everyone's phone in town.

Like a lot of small towns across America, the fire station is the center of activity. Pancake breakfasts and a side of local gossip are the norm. Funding is usually tight for a small-town department, so they have to be active in keeping the department in operating money. Our volunteer fire department hosted an annual "Homecoming" fair at the fire station. There were all the goodies: cotton candy, candied apples, and funnel cake. The carnies would set up a few rides like the Tilt-A-Whirl and an old-fashioned carousel. My dad helped run all of the electrical wiring and set up the game and cooking booths.

It was our big fundraiser to keep equipment.

The Ladies Auxiliary made some imagine! There was a dunk tank, ri other fun things to do. A huge p through the town square and past spend hours waxing all of the rig the public. I used to ride with my out to all the screaming kids on th marching band, the Boy Scouts an firefighters and Ladies Auxiliary m parade also. I couldn't wait for it e great slice of Americana.

For the years through element school, I went with my dad on all a great experience. Our fire depa program for sixteen year olds. I could get my driver's license and monthly meeting after my sixteent the other members. I had waited f

The department started gettin school every day a couple of us w the pumper. The department had through the Comprehensive Em (CETA) federal work program. So called "Q Ball" because of his sh be a driver on each shift, every da with me. If there was a fire call school immediately and dash acr

to ge
where
haire
allow
to be
cours

Q
and la
appar
masks
lot of
workir
all of t
trainin
house
fancy n

Unf
1976. H
someho
serious
in the
he had
The ph
took the
the free
we had
time I jo
up hose
the fire

With mom and dad around 1972

I grew up skating on the local ponds each winter and started to play hockey with the neighborhood gang. We had an official ice rink at the local park. I skated there every weekend, and we started a local hockey league. In high school I skated with my best friend, Tom, for a team of high school players at Kent State University. It sure made winter pass by quicker!

1977, almost my draft year! How could the NHL pass on a 155-pound defenseman?

We owned a small trailer and would go camping every summer. My dad was an only kid, but my mom had two brothers and three sisters. We would often go visit them, including a big trip out to California to visit her brothers and their families. My grandma lived with us; her husband died when my mom was young, so we made an apartment for her when we built our new house in 1964. All my mom's side of the family would often make the pilgrimage back to visit. My other grandparents lived close by across the state line in a small steel town. My grandfather poured hot steel five days a week at a local mill. He worked his ass off every single day for forty-five years. I was their only grandkid, so they always brought the best presents at Christmas. My grandfather always called me "boy."

This is Fred William Grimm, my grandfather that poured hot steel for over four decades at the same steel mill.

room. Every single rest stop we were at had the men's on the right and the women's on the left. Well, all of them are the same except for this one. They were reversed. So out of habit I just bolted into the door on the right without looking.

My parents were actually worried. My dad had been looking for me in the men's room and my mom was wandering around the parking lot calling my name. They actually did think I was kidnapped.

They had a great laugh over it all when we got back in the car, and, of course, couldn't wait to humiliate me in front of Aunt Betty and Uncle Mel with the story.

I was scarred for life.

To this day, I double and triple check the doors to make sure I use the correct bathroom in all public places!

THE TAG ALONG

My dad loved to go camping. We started out with a pop-up tent trailer and would go all over to the various lakes and forests in Ohio and Pennsylvania each summer. It was a great way to spend summertime, and we would do the usual: hike, s'mores, hot dogs over the open fire, bicycle riding, and ghost stories with other kids at the campground. All of the usual camping items were checked off the list each summer.

My dad wanted to move up and get a bigger trailer. He sold the tent trailer and purchased a little tagalong trailer. It was a great deal from someone he knew. It just needed a little work. He bought it in the fall and spent hours all winter, out in the freezing Ohio weather, to get it ready for the spring. He put in a new oven and stove and installed a fold-down bed for me. He put new cabinets in and a new floor covering. The trailer was looking fantastic.

It was the summer of 1975, and I was fifteen. My dad decided to put it at a campground for the summer. We would stay there for about eight weeks, only about fifteen miles from our house. He would drive to work from the campground each hang with him on a Friday night. I could sleep over and be there to go on calls. Sure, that sounded great. I asked my dad if I could spend the night. He didn't have any problems with it, as he knew I had been to a lot of emergencies and would enjoy the experience. I saw Billy before school that morning as I put my gear on the pumper. There were four of us that got out of school to go on fire calls during the day. I let him know I would be by after school. We made plans to get a couple of huge hoagie sandwiches for dinner.

We hung out that evening, laughing and playing cards. A couple of the other guys stopped in. Friday's at the fire station were sort of a social event. Guys would stop in and say hi and shoot the breeze for a while. We usually ended up playing a few games of Euchre. Everyone had finally gone home, since it was getting late.

The station had two big bay doors and a number of fire trucks parked in the apparatus area. My turnout gear was on the first-line pumper, but I wanted to put it next to my bed, so I could get it on right away if we had a call. The plan was for Billy to drive, of course, and I would ride the tailboard, the back step of the pumper. There was a safety strap that hooked around on the bar above the hose bed. The trick to riding the tailboard was to keep your knees bent. If we had a fire, I would wrap the fire hydrant with the supply hose, hook it up, and get water to Billy, and then attack the fire.

Simple stuff. Right?

The fire station had a direct telephone line to it. There was no 911 system back then in town, so citizens had to call the seven-digit number. The fire phone, as we called it, was hooked up to a speaker and a very loud horn. If there was a fire, Billy would start the pumper and then hit the emergency-call switch. That started the giant air-raid-type siren on the roof of the station and got the beacon tower red light going. He would then put out on the radio what the emergency call was and where. Then off we would go, Billy driving like Mario Andretti, with me on the tailboard, speeding to the rescue. This was all some glamorous stuff for a seventeen-year-old!

I put my fire boots and bunker pants next to my bed. My coat and helmet were next to the dorm room door. I had the safety strap unhooked, ready to jump on the tailboard and hook myself in. Everything was set. I was really tired that evening. I had a long day at school and had endless laps and wind sprints at track team practice before showing up. For dinner we had eaten two hoagies each; my stomach was full of cold cuts and bread. As I settled in bed, I was exhausted. Billy was already snoring. I drifted off to sleep in seconds.

HOOOOOOONK!

The fire phone rang at about three in the morning. Billy jumped up and started talking. A man was frantically yelling his garage was on fire. Billy dashed to the office and put out the radio call to all of the volunteers. The roof top siren started its big, loud wail to alert the volunteers. It was so loud that it shook the firehouse.

Do you remember when you were a teenager and how hard it was to wake up? Do you remember how hard it is to see when you first wake up and a bright light is on? Your eyes

LESSONS LEARNED

Being on the volunteer fire department was an incredible learning experience. At the time, I didn't realize it, but I was being guided in the right directions in my life by a lot of different people from all walks of life.

Q Ball was an incredibly patient man. Here he was trying to serve the township with himself and three young full-time firefighters, plus the older men that were on the department, and the handful of young high schoolers like myself.

One day we had a house fire that had fire blowing out of every single window when we arrived. It was a weekday, so only the couple of us that got out of school were there, plus two or three of the older guys that had jobs in town that they could leave. We stretched a couple of attack lines and got it knocked down quickly, but there was a lot of damage done. It was a two-story home. The roof had fallen in and the back wall was collapsed into the yard. We were surprised the fire got such a head start on us, as it was the middle of the day and surely people had seen the smoke. However, this was before every person on the planet had a cell phone, so we assumed many people just thought someone was burning garbage or leaves.

We spent a couple of hours digging through what we could to get all of the hot spots put out. (There's nothing more embarrassing than putting a fire out and then having to come back that night because it flared up again.) Q Ball told us to take a break. A couple of us sat on the sidewalk and drank some water and soft drinks.

Q Ball marched toward us quickly . . .

"Get the hell off of the sidewalk and sit over there!" he yelled.

"Why, Chief?"

"Just shut up and do it. Now!"

We picked up our gear and drinks and moved to the yard where he pointed to for us to sit and rehab.

"What the hell is wrong with him?" one of the guys muttered under his breath.

We all just looked at each other and shrugged.

About five minutes later, the giant chimney came crashing down, strewing high speed bricks all over where we had just been sitting on the sidewalk.

"Damn! Q Ball knows his stuff and probably just saved our lives!" I blurted out to the other guys.

Q Ball looked over at where we were sitting with a "I know what I'm doing" glare. We all got up and scurried around to find something to do to avoid his wrath.

The next training session covered fireground safety. I think Q Ball enjoyed showing us young kids the ropes. He never stopped teaching us. The chimney collapse was "Exhibit A" of that session.

Q Ball started to get really cranky, however. He started losing his cool with all of us. We wondered what was going on with him.

Then we found out. "Mrs. Chief," his lovely wife, was dying of cancer. It all started to make sense. She went quickly, which was a blessing, as she was very ill. Q Ball asked me and a few of the other younger firefighters to be pallbearers at her funeral. What an honor for us.

Growing up in that little rural town was a kid's dream. From my Pop Warner football coaches to teachers and others, it really was a village raising its kids. I was on the high school track team and playing hockey. I saved up and had my own car: a 1961 Pontiac Tempest, and then a Plymouth Scamp. Real hot rods! I got to run into burning buildings, sometimes even with my dad. We had great neighbors on that gravel road. It truly was like living in some TV show like *The Andy Griffith Show*.

I worked at a local farm that had a craft shop on the premises when I was twelve. I helped stock the warehouse, but mostly I went out and helped the owner, "Boss," to cut down trees and make lumber at his sawmill. I guess I moved pretty slow, because he called me "Flash." It's where I learned to drive tractors and a bulldozer. His two sons also built a track in the field for dirt bikes in the summer and snowmobile racing in the winter. I worked there with a classmate named

Galen. We had a lot of fun back then. But damn did we work hard for fifty cents an hour!

I moved on to the sporting goods store over the hill in the steel town in PA. That was a great job, and the store was owned by a wonderful family. They treated me so well. It was across the street from the city firehouse that I visited with my dad often, so the firefighters that worked there would come in to see me when their kids needed a new baseball mitt or uniforms for gym class the local schools required.

As my high school graduation and my eighteenth birthday approached, I knew I wanted more out of life. My Uncle Jim, who had moved to California years earlier, came home my senior year for a visit. Everyone thought my grandma that lived with us was dying. She wasn't, and went on to live ten more years. I told Uncle Jim I needed to come to California. He agreed that I could stay with him and his wife, my Aunt Wilma. What an offer. I hardly knew my California relatives; this was going to be quite an exciting experience.

I saved up as much money as I could and sold the Scamp. Like all kids my age, I watched the television show *Emergency!*. I think that show prodded an entire generation to be firefighters, nurses, or doctors. I was motivated.

My goal was to get on a fire department in Southern California, just like Johnny and Roy.

I graduated from high school on a beautiful May Saturday, and the very next Saturday, a few weeks from my eighteenth birthday, I was on a plane to California.

My first job there was working at the old West Covina Ice Arena. I handed out skates, patrolled the ice, and drove the Zamboni. It was the perfect job for a rink rat like me. I bought an old Honda 350 street bike to get around on. I was also refereeing the adult hockey league games and played some games in the Senior A Pacific Coast Hockey League, which was basically *Slap Shot*-style goon mayhem with a few goals mixed in.

The owner of the rink, Joe, liked to give me the crappy jobs. Cleaning out the old compressor room was like being in an oil field. But he would always throw me an extra $100 cash after a job like that.

One night I was riding my Honda out to the rink with my gear bag strapped down to the back and my hockey sticks sticking straight up, strapped to the frame and gear bag. I hurried out of the house; it was kind of chilly that night. I had on my high school hockey jacket, some jeans and sneakers, and my big white helmet. What a sight, I suppose.

As I approached Kellogg Hill on I-10 by Pomona, I started slowing, as the bike was pretty gutless. I looked in my mirrors and holy crap . . . About fifty motorcycles were coming my way.

Now remember, this is 1978, maybe the height of biker gangs in SoCal. I squeezed some more throttle, but I just started slowing more.

My mind started racing. Here I am, a million miles away from the safety of that Ohio gravel road. I look like a complete geek, with hockey sticks to boot!

They got closer.

All I could think about was one of them would ride up next to me and kick my front wheel and put me down. I was scared shitless. My heart was pounding out of my chest.

They caught up to me. Some swerved to the right of me and some started to pass on the left.

I was shaking.

The first biker pulls up right next to me. This dude was the typical biker. Big, bare armed, beard flowing, colors on.

He just looked at me, up and down. I nodded to him. He flashed me a peace sign and off he motored.

All 50 or so of the bikes rumbled past me. Each guy or gal just nodded or smiled. I was so relieved. Off they went, up the hill and down with ease, all in a group. I don't know where they were off to, as it was a Sunday night, but I didn't care. I bought a little Toyota Corolla a few weeks later.

I had a great time at my Aunt Wilma and Uncle Jim's house. I got to know my cousins Cliff and Janice well and started to finally not be so homesick. Cliff had a motorcycle also, so we would go on rides and always end up at Pup 'N' Taco for lunch. Those were always great afternoons.

I took a couple of fire department tests. They were harder than I thought they would be. The best I did was finishing number sixty-one out of about five thousand applicants with the Pomona Fire Department. Pretty good for a teenager. But in the interview, I did well, but my age kept coming up, and

I knew it was going to be an issue with every department I tested with.

I left the Zamboni for a better paying job. I was hired as a manager trainee at a company called Best Products. They assigned me to the warehouse. Best Products was a catalog-showroom-type store. They had one item on display in the different departments. Housewares, sporting goods, toys, and a jewelry department were on the ground floor. When a customer wanted to buy the items, they would fill out a form and shoot it up to the warehouse upstairs by a pneumatic-tube system. An entire team of runners would fill the orders and put them on a big conveyor belt that went down to the pick-up area. It was the worst job I ever had. By a million miles the worst! I worked ridiculously long hours for little pay. Retail sucked.

One thing came out of working there that was good. I met Randy, the assistant manager in the toy department. He was a few years older than I , but we hit it off instantly. I also have two other wonderful friends from working there, Paulette and DeLynn, both were cashiers. When we get together now, we all laugh about those long-ago days. They were the only three good things about that job.

I was growing frustrated with my lack of progress getting hired on a fire department. I finally had my own apartment with a roommate, a street bike, a dirt bike, and a little Toyota Corolla, but the fire department thing just wasn't working out. And if I worked a few more weeks at Best Products with my horrible boss, I was probably going to go postal!

UNCLE BOB

My Uncle Bob was quite the character. He was a hell-raiser as a kid, was in the CCC camps, joined the Army at seventeen, and had the spirit of adventure burning inside of him.

Uncle Bob planning an adventure in his early '60s

I would stop over in Glendora once in a while to visit Uncle Bob and Aunt Mid. Uncle Bob was always working on his ham radios, his motorcycles, or his cars. I think he had a computer before anyone in our family. He loved gadgets and tinkering. He also loved the outdoors.

One day I stopped in and he asked if I wanted to go on an overnight backpacking trip.

"Sure, sounds fun," I said.

We made plans to go on an overnight hike up to the Santa Anita Canyon and hike the Sturtevant Falls trail the following weekend.

A week later I met Uncle Bob at his house. I had asked him if I needed to bring anything, but he said he had it all covered. We drove up to the ranger station at Chantry Flat, parked the car, signed in at the office, and off we went.

It was summertime, and it was a pretty hot day. I was eighteen years old and in great shape; Uncle Bob was fifty-seven. He was motoring up the trail like a damn billy goat! We stopped at the falls and cooled off, putting our feet in the chilly mountain water. We continued up the trail quite a way. He knew of a spot to set up our tents that was by a little stream at the top of the canyon. We finally made it and set up camp. We had our tiny one-person tents set up in no time and then all of a sudden . . .

The ground started rumbling for a few seconds.

"Was that an earthquake, Uncle Bob!" said the kid from Ohio that had never, ever been in an earthquake before.

"Yup," he said calmly.

"We should go back down and make sure everyone is OK."

I was really thinking that all of Los Angeles had just fallen down. I only knew earthquakes as devastating. It was only a few years after the Sylmar quake, and of course I had just seen the movie *Earthquake*.

Uncle Bob calmed me down. He said it was no big deal. I laugh now when I think about it. I really did think all LA was reduced to rubble. Hey, I grew up where we had tornadoes, not earthquakes. What did I know!

Night fell and my stomach started grumbling. When you're eighteen, you eat a lot and are always hungry.

"What's for dinner Uncle Bob?"

"Here ya go, kid!" He tossed me a bag of little Tootsie Rolls and some trail mix. "There's your dinner."

Are you kidding me?

"Haha, real funny, Unc, what are we really having for dinner?"

"That's it," he said, laughing.

"You have to keep your backpack light to hike efficiently."

He said he never took much to eat, as he didn't want to be weighed down, and it was only an overnight hike. As I ate the candy, my stomach only grumbled more. And then, to add insult to injury, two hikers showed up and pitched a tent by the creek next to us. They said hello, but then kept to themselves. And then it happened: they brought out a six pack of Coors and started cooking two giant steaks over their campfire!

The smell of their steaks was killing me.

Uncle Bob was a Mormon, so there was no ice-cold beer in our backpacks. I ate a handful of trail mix and just started laughing. Note to self: Next time I hike with Uncle Bob, I'm bringing the food.

The stars were shining brightly and the smell of the pine trees was invigorating. It was great to be high above the summertime smog in such fresh air. I dozed off, wondering if anything really did fall down in LA.

In the morning, we woke up to the smell of the pines, the fresh air and the birds singing (and a sore back from sleeping in the tent). We took down our "camp" and started to head way back down to the car.

We got to the falls; it was really a searing hot day. Uncle Bob said, "Let's jump in and cool off!"

He stripped down to his underwear and jumped in. Well, I was roasting, so I did the same.

So here is this skinny eighteen-year-old swimming and laughing with this bearded old fart, in their underwear, not far from Hollywood. You can imagine the sight and what someone might think.

Just then I heard some sounds of kids approaching.

What the . . .

And lots of them!

An entire class of fifth graders was hiking up the trail with their teacher and a few parent chaperones. The little bastards just looked at us and started laughing.

The water in the pool at the base of the falls was freezing, but I got in under the water as far as I could. So did Uncle Bob. We were shivering like crazy, in about five feet of icy mountain water, while all of these school kids started splashing at the edge to cool off.

The teacher gave us an odd look. Like one of those long, disapproving "I know what you two perverts are up to" looks! We kept submerged as much as possible, but I know she could see us in our tighty-whities.

How embarrassing.

Finally, after what seemed like an eternity, but I'm sure was only about a minute or two, the teacher rounded up the kids and headed up the trail. We jumped out of the pond and got on shore, freezing and shivering. We looked at each other and just started laughing our asses off.

We put our clothes back on when we finally dried and beelined it back down the trail. I was relieved when we got back to civilization and every building was still standing.

We went right to a Shakey's Pizza for the all you can eat "Bunch of Lunch." Nice try, Uncle Bob, but I knew you were starving your butt off up there too.

What a character!

He would have been one hundred years young on the day I'm writing this story.

BACK EAST IT IS

I was growing frustrated with the fire department testing in Southern California. I was having fun, but I was starting to miss my friends I grew up with. My job at Best Products was a nowhere position. You could tell that even the store manager and assistant managers hated their jobs. I had been in California for almost a year without getting close to a fire-department job.

My dad called to let me know that the city fire department in Pennsylvania was going to hire seven new firefighters. The hometown volunteer department was also going to hire three more firefighters, as their call volume was picking up and it was getting harder to get volunteers to respond to daytime emergencies. He told me that Q Ball even asked about me, to see if I was going to ever move back. I figured that was pretty good news.

I'm not a big fan of winter, but I knew I needed some more experience—well, a LOT more experience, and I knew I needed to be older to get hired on a department in California. It was a hard decision to leave, but I sold the Toyota to my cousin

Janice and gave my motorcycles to my roommate, to keep in case I came back. My cousin Lewis had just moved back to Ohio, and he had a car that needed to be driven back. I told him I would gladly drive it for him. I tossed my clothes and hockey gear in his Honda and off I went. I drove it with just one stop, in Amarillo, Texas, to see if they would remove the nine stiches in my lip from a wayward puck that had hit me in my last PCHL game.

I returned home, and Mom and Dad were of course happy to have me. They were never too fond of me living in SoCal and riding motorcycles. After a few days, I couldn't take being there, as I was used to my freedom, and they still viewed me as a senior in high school. I moved into a tent trailer at my friend Tom's house. We picked right back up playing hockey together and having fun. I applied at the steel town's full-time fire department, and I gave my application in person to Q Ball at the volunteer department. He gave me my old turnout gear and added me back to the volunteer "active" roster.

I was pretty excited about my chances. Q Ball knew me since I was about six years old, and the chief of the city fire department in Pennsylvania, "Old Dad," knew me since I was born. His son, PT, was a good friend of mine, and their family went to the same church as my family. My father went to high school with Old Dad. I figured I was in a pretty good situation with both fire departments.

Q Ball scheduled an interview with me. There was also going to be a township trustee sitting in on the interviews. When I arrived at the fire station, I smiled when I looked at the hydrant in front of the station that I had painted two years

The East Side firehouse, the alarm desk entrance is on the right

I came in to work one day after a late night out with my hockey buddies. We had played a game at the Kent State ice rink and stayed out way too late, as usual. Artie, the shift captain, told me to pack up and go drive to East Side for Red, the lieutenant, because his usual firefighter partner was on vacation. I was happy about that, as Red was a great guy and was fun to work for. I rolled in and put my gear on the Mack pumper, ready to face the day.

The East Side firehouse was built by the Works Progress Administration (WPA) workers during the depression. It had two narrow bays and the pumper's mirrors just barely cleared the doors. We had to back in, so it really tested your driving skills. It was on a very busy intersection in town, and Old Dad lived across the street. On the main floor there was the apparatus area, that housed the Mack and an old 1940s era pumper that was turned into a foam truck for the magnesium fires at the mills. In the front there was a small office with a desk and the old ticker tape machine. We had pull-box alarms throughout the city, and the ticker tape would punch out the box number as the big gong would beat out the numbers also. We always had to keep the ticker tape wound so it would work.

There was no 911 telephone system then, so we had a station phone and the bright red seven-digit fire phone. The pole room had lockers for everyone's safety gear and the big rubber mat for the pole to cushion the slide. The pole room was right behind the front office. There was a small bathroom and shower and a tiny kitchen in the very back. The upstairs had these narrow rickety wooden steps that lead to a small bathroom, two beds, and a TV area with two recliners. There was a door on the "pole hole" so no one would accidently fall. It wasn't much, but it was by far my favorite firehouse I've ever worked at. It had character. There was also a basement, as it was built on the steep side of a gully. No one ever wanted to go down into that dark dungeon.

Red greeted me in the office. We chatted a bit, then I checked out the rig and the air levels on our breathing apparatus. He asked me if I really knew how to drive a pumper, so we went out for a cruise around town. He grilled me on some street locations and had me hook up to a hydrant and do some pumping. When we got back to the firehouse, he showed me the trick to backing the pumper in, by aligning it with the telephone pole across the street. His tips made it so much easier and more efficient. There were always a number of cars stopped at the busy intersection when we had to back in, so the pressure was on in front of such a large audience to not screw it up.

food. Well, of course the city wasn't

lk out and put the towel back in the
ay their orders.

thirty minutes, the prisoners would start
screaming at the officers, demanding to
ffee, sunny side up eggs with bacon, and

. The cops never thought that was as funny

Later that morning, Red told me he was going upstairs to "study." He had also been out a bit late after golfing the previous day. He asked me to keep an eye out for Old Dad, as he stopped in every shift. I told him not to worry and I would holler up when Old Dad arrived in the chief's car.

"No, you dumbass, shake the pole so he can't hear you!"

"OK, Red, I'm on it!"

Red went upstairs; I grabbed the newspaper and sat at the alarm desk. I made sure the ticker tape was wound and opened the front door to let the summer breeze in. I was reading the paper and watching the cars drive by. I had my feet up on the desk and then . . .

"Hey Grimmy, where's Red?"

Oh God, Oh God! It's Old Dad, right in front of me.

I had fallen asleep hard at the alarm desk. I didn't know what to do. Here I'm on probation and I'm asleep. Red gave me one job to do and I blew it.

"I'm not sure, Chief, I think he's upstairs."

My mind was racing. You dumbass, tell him he's in the kitchen in the back, not upstairs. What was I thinking! I could have hit the pole as we walked back to the kitchen looking for him.

The chief walked up the creaking steps slowly.

He caught Red in bed, under the covers, snoring away.

I heard their mumbled conversation. Well, at least there was no yelling, so that's good, right? The chief came down the stairs and walked right by without saying goodbye. He was pissed. Then I heard the old, rickety wooden stairs creaking again. Here comes Red. Oh Shit. And then he appears in the office, looking at me with squinty eyes.

"Grimmy, I gave you *one* job, just *one* job . . .

YOU DUMBASS!"

"I'm sorry Red . . . the . . . well . . . I . . . um . . . I fell asleep because I was out way late last night!"

Red just started laughing.

"Grimmy, you can't fly like an eagle if you're gonna be out hootin' like an owl."

And that was it. He just strolled back to the kitchen to get something to eat.

Whew.

at the mouth for some
feeding them!

He would then wa
kitchen and throw aw

In about twenty or
banging on the bars,
know where their co
toast were.

It's kind of weird
as we did.

The old
the city
for the fire eq
the police stati
departments ha
dry fire hoses wa
station. You coul
area that led right

Every once in a w
be full of people th
disorderly Saturday n
that the pokey was kir
get a notepad and pen,
in and ask the guys in tl
breakfast. He would ask
they wanted their eggs co
would like. All the hung

THE DIET

66 Hey guys, I'm on this new diet and it really seems to be working," the captain told us.

We all just looked up at him then kept eating our breakfast. Everyone on duty knew he wasn't' on some new diet, because he was eating everything in sight. And, he was so prone to being full of horse manure, constantly telling elaborate stories no one ever believed.

The crew had to hear this diet talk every shift for about three weeks. We all could see he wasn't losing a pound. It actually was getting comical, as we thought he looked like he was actually gaining weight.

Enough was enough. We swiped all his uniform pants out of his locker and had one of the firefighter's wives stitch them in about half an inch. The altered pants were put back in his locker before his next shift. We all crowded in at shift change to watch him struggle to get them zipped up. His excuses were hilarious!

"I think the dryer is shrinking these work pants!"

We were all fighting hard to keep a straight face.

He went out and bought some new pants, and of course, those ended up getting hemmed after hearing nonstop about his diet. He was hilarious to watch as he tried to suck in his gut to get them on every morning at shift change in front of everyone piled in the locker room to watch.

The captain came in the next shift and announced that his diet had worked, and his doctor told him he was in fantastic shape for his age and could now eat anything.

Miraculously all his pants were opened up by about three inches and he had to use his belt to tighten them his next shift.

"See!" he said, as he easily slipped into his work pants. "This diet has worked wonders!"

I QUIT SMOKING

Tom was a real character. He was usually the Houseman at the downtown station. He sat at the firehouse kitchen table stuffing envelopes for hours. He would send in every single coupon, call in to every single radio show and always try to win free stuff. He would enter hundreds of contests per day. I think he must have spent more on postage than anyone I've ever known.

He was also a couple of packs a day smoker. He would stamp a few contest entries and then head out to the apparatus room for a smoke a couple of times per day.

One shift he came into the firehouse and announced he had quit smoking. The crew asked him how he was doing it: Was he chewing that gross gum? or quitting cold turkey? Tom had just gotten married and had a baby on the way. He wasn't the healthiest person and had some heart troubles in the past. He told us he was just quitting cold turkey.

Well, no one ever gets away with anything at the firehouse. If someone is up to something, there is no way to hide it from everyone else. It's just that simple. We all live together for twenty-four hours. There really are no secrets.

Tom's crew knew he really hadn't quit. In the evenings he would sneak out behind the firehouse and light up and puff away. But when asked, he still stuck to his story that he had quit.

One shift Luke stopped in at the novelty shop downtown. They sold all sorts of fun stuff, such as magic trick supplies. He bought a pack of cigarette loads. Remember them? You put them in a cigarette and they would explode when smoked.

Luke found Tom's pack of smokes and "loaded" them all.

The crew was in the TV room watching a movie that evening.

POP!

The sound of a cigarette blowing up came from the back of the station. Everyone starting cracking up, but had to pull it together before Tom walked back in. The door from the apparatus bay opens and in walks a very red-faced Tom. He knew that he had been pranked by the best. He just walked through to the locker room, without saying a word— probably to change his underwear!

The next shift, Tom strolled in, and while everyone was at the kitchen table having morning coffee, he put his pack of cigarettes down in front of him and announced that he had taken up smoking again.

TIMMY COCONUTS

The city I worked for was like most small Pennsylvania steel towns. A river ran through a downtown shopping area, and meandered down towards the Ohio River, lined with huge steel and pipe mills belching smoke daily. There was a nice downtown area with restaurants, small shops, banks, and, of course, an Army Navy Store, a staple in all small towns in the area.

The people that lived there were a hard-working bunch. The lunch pail types. I remember going with my grandma in the old Dodge Dart to drop off or pick up my grandpa at the mill he worked at. Those employees just trudged out after every shift, dirty and tired. This scene was played out across town at the various mills and factories daily.

Politics are also a big deal in a town like that. I was actually surprised when I got hired, because I was from "across the state line," an Ohio kid. One of the city councilmen would let me know about it too, every time he saw me! The politicians only wanted city residents getting city jobs.

The city had seven firefighters per shift. We would often get down to only five when there were vacations or sick call ins. We really needed everyone to be able to pull their own weight at a fire. We all had to know how to operate the pumpers and the hundred-foot aerial ladder. Everyone really had to pull their own weight and work hard at calls.

So, what happened next is surprising, but also not!

One day a short, chubby guy with a curly perm and Coke bottle glasses walked into the downtown firehouse. He had one of our uniforms on. What the . . .? Who is this guy? We all looked at each other in bewilderment. Old Dad, the fire chief, came out of his office and shook his hand. They both walked over to the fire engine we were washing.

"Hi boys, this is our new fireman, Timmy Coconuts."

"Hello," Timmy said quietly, while he shook the captain's hand.

We all said hello and shook his hand. Old Dad ushered him into the office to fill out some paperwork and give him his badge and safety gear.

"Are you fucking kidding me?" The captain couldn't believe his eyes.

"We just hired a five-foot-five bowling ball!"

"Well, soon enough we'll find out who he's related to," I muttered.

All of the guys laughed. That was it! He just *had* to be related to the mayor or a councilman— *had* to!

Timmy left in his lime green Volkswagen "Thing" after getting all of his safety gear. Old Dad assigned him to shift 3, which was pretty much a band of department misfits already, so he would probably fit right in.

The captain couldn't take it anymore and went in to Old Dad's office later that afternoon. He was pretty pissed off. He just had to know how or why we hired this fellow. He was so short I don't think he could reach the ladder racks on the side of the pumper.

Well, it turns out I was almost correct in my assumption of his hiring. Close but no cigar though.

He was a death bed promise.

Bill Sherman had been the mayor for three terms. He was running for reelection and was posting his signs around the city. There was a street in town that the Little League baseball field was on. It had a sharp turn at the field. If you went right, you were in the parking lot and left, you continued down the street. Right on that corner was a house owned by Timmy's widowed mother. She had never, ever allowed a politician to put a sign up in her yard. They all wanted to, however, as it was a great location for many of the city's residents to see a big sign. Mayor Sherman always stopped in and said hello to Mrs. Coconuts. He had the city workers shovel her walk of snow and kept the trees in her yard trimmed. He schmoozed her with chocolate from the local shop and with Christmas and birthday cards. She still said no.

One day the mayor stopped by to try and convince her about the sign and rang the doorbell. A nurse answered the door.

It turns out that Mrs. Coconuts was diagnosed with terminal cancer. The mayor went in and met with her in the bedroom. He had now forgotten all about putting his sign in her yard. He genuinely felt sorrow as he held her hand and they quietly talked.

"Mayor," she said weakly.

"Yes, Mrs. Coconuts"

"Would you like to put your sign in my yard?"

"Oh, Mrs. Coconuts, that's not important right now."

"Yes, it is, Mayor. I want you to do me a favor."

"Whatever you need," the mayor whispered.

"Do you remember my son, Timmy?"

"Of course, I do."

"He wants to be a policeman, Mayor. Really badly."

"Did he take the last civil service test?"

"Yes, he passed it with a really good score, but the city didn't hire him."

"I'll look into it for you, Mrs. Coconuts."

"Thanks mayor, you can put a sign in my yard too."

Timmy's mom passed away a few weeks later. There was a giant "Bill Sherman for Mayor" billboard in the front yard the day after the funeral.

When the mayor told the police chief he wanted Timmy hired, it was no big deal. Department heads were used to

e's steering wheel rubbed onto his uniform shirt
all stain. We called it the "Richard Petty Rub"
ous NASCAR driver).

called to a dumpster-fire call their first shift
Timmy grinded the gears all the way there.
led the fire engine into the alleyway and got it into
e, and they put out the burning trash quickly. On
to the station, Timmy was going through all of
oothly. The Night Commander wondered what felt
e the rig wasn't really getting any power. Timmy
n to take the pumper out of "Pump" mode and to
nto drive. The engine was working the pump only,
he drive train, all the way down the hill. No power
to the wheels! He had coasted it down the alley
e steep street with zero power to the drive train.

wasn't really suited to be on the fire department,
such a nice guy, everyone really tried hard to get
speed on the equipment and raising ladders and
He was a work in progress for sure!

side story about the Night Commander: Years later,
nging the ladder truck back from a call and backing
downtown station. The department had just taken
f a brand-new pumper. It wasn't in service yet, as
were still mounting some equipment and getting
or action. The aerial ladder was a midship mount—
the turntable the mechanical ladder is attached to
behind the cab, and the ladder points to the rear of
. The ladder sticks out quite a bit from the chassis.
acked in, he forgot *all* about the new pumper, and

being told who to hire, until he met Timmy in person. The police chief called up to the Mayor's office and said no way in hell was he hiring a nearly blind, five-foot-five, 240-pound policeman.

That's when Timmy got sent to the fire chief. Old Dad, being the good fire chief and person that he was, never wanted to upset the apple cart with the long serving mayor.

Welcome to the fire service Timmy Coconuts!

THE NIGHT COMMANDER

One of my very best friends and favorite people to ever work with is the "Night Commander." Steve got that name as a result of a newspaper article. I was working at the East Side firehouse one evening when there was this HUGE boom. The two front apparatus bay doors shook like crazy.

What the . . .?

The East Side firehouse is on the corner of one of the busiest intersections in town, so I thought a car had crashed into the station.

Instantly, the fire phone started ringing off of the hook, as this was still in the pre-911 days. A house about fifteen blocks away from us just literally blew up!

The department had been getting busier with fires. The mills were laying off people as the steel industry of 1980 was circling the drain. Laid off workers couldn't make their house payments, so they started burning them for the insurance money.

When we arrived, th
and most of the walls w
a block away. Luckily, n
as they would have been

The fire sort of blew i
was some junk smolderin
dug through the rubble f
when it exploded. Luckily

We called in the fire
Marshall's Office to handle
and made an arrest in abou
holes in the walls and filled i
until all of it ignited at once

If we would have been c
probably been killed in the e

The local newspaper rep
Steve. They quoted him as bein
and of course from then on,
Commander.

When Steve was promoted t
if I could be sent to his shift to
I reluctantly agreed to go to his
end up working with another
Timmy Coconuts! The Night Con
East Side, he would rarely have t

I took a few days off for vacatio
East Side to drive. The Night Comr
his driving and pumping skills each

the fire engin
and left a sm
(after the fam

They wer
together, an
Timmy whee
"Pump" mod
the way bac
the gears sm
different, li
had forgotte
put it back i
bypassing t
was getting
and onto th

Timmy
but he was
him up to
hose pulls

A quick
he was br
it into the
delivery
the crew
it ready
meaning
sits righ
the truc
As he b

smashed in the windshield. It had to go back to the factory for repairs before it ever ran a call. No one was back there helping him.

I would have expected that out of Timmy.

What a dumbass!

MR. WIZARD

The Mr. Wizard prank is one of my firehouse favorites. We pulled it on Timmy Coconuts and a couple of the other newer firefighters.

We told him that Red had this amazing friend that won all sorts of money in Las Vegas; his friend was a man of mystery that could predict events. We could even shuffle a deck of cards, Timmy could pick one, and Mr. Wizard would tell him *exactly* what card he had just picked, over the phone, all the way from Nevada!

One day at lunch we built up the patter. Mr. Wizard was a "know all" kind of savant with great mind power. We told Timmy that he could shuffle any deck of cards he wanted and cut the cards in half, then Mr. Wizard, over the phone, would tell him exactly what card he had picked.

Timmy was skeptical, but he agreed to try it. We found a deck of cards and Timmy shuffled them up. We said not to pick his card until we called, so no one could tip off Mr. Wizard. The entire crew sat there in the firehouse kitchen so that he knew no one was somehow cheating.

what they had just encountered! Inspection was over for the day.

No wonder Old Joe worked there for so many years!

Who ever said fire inspections are boring?

OLD DAD

Old Dad had been the chief of the department for just a couple months when he hired me in 1979. There had been a member of his family on the job since the fire department was started in the early 1900s. He was a great guy and a LOT of fun at parties. The guy could put his Irish heritage to work and gulp down an entire pitcher of beer in about one second!

He was also a terrific guy to deal with as chief, and he really valued all of the members of the department. However, Old Dad had the tendency to sometimes get a little overexcited on fire calls and other stressful situations.

The downtown firehouse with the yellow pumper and red ladder truck.
The mayor's office was right above the giant bay door.

There's a bridge in downtown on the main street over the river. On each side there's a tall flagpole in the center of the bridge. Whenever there was an event in town, the hosting organizations wanted us to use our ladder truck to put up the banners and stretch them from pole to pole across the bridge. We did this most of the time, even in the freezing cold of winter. We were all about community service; however, we didn't have many firefighters on duty each shift to protect the city, and the last thing we needed was to be stuck on the bridge with the ladder truck up in the air, with two firefighters out of service until they could get it down.

Red became our union president and decided this was a pretty bad policy. He approached Old Dad and said we weren't going to do this any longer, because it was a detriment to the safety of the department and main street in downtown and to the safety of the residents. The city street department had a small bucket truck that was available to use if needed and would be a much safer alternative.

The United Way came to the downtown firehouse with their annual fundraiser banner. Old Dad asked the on-duty crew to take it over to the bridge and hang it. The captain told him no, it wasn't going to be put up by his on-duty crew as this was already discussed between the chief and the union president and agreed upon.

A heated discussion ensued and Old Dad stormed off.

Fine! He was just going to do it himself.

The chief jumped in the ladder truck and took off for the bridge. To operate a ladder truck like this, it took using the controls on the pedestal at the base of the ladder to move it up, down, in, or out and swing it around in either direction. There are two big "feet" on each side of the unit, called outriggers, that need to be put out manually so the ladder truck has more stability and won't tip over when the ladder is in use.

Old Dad parked the ladder truck in the middle of the bridge. He put down the outriggers by hand and locked them in with the safety pins. Now he had to "fly" the ladder up to the first flag pole. The chief climbed up the twenty or so feet to attach it to the one side. Then he had to climb back down and rotate the ladder and fly it to the other flag pole. This was taking some time, and Old Dad was getting more pissed off on every climb. When he finally got the banner tied and straight after about an hour and a half, he put up the outriggers and was finished.

Now luckily, the city had just buried many of the power and phone lines underground in the downtown area. Because what happened next was amazing.

You see, Old Dad, in all of his frustration and haste, had started driving back to the firehouse with the ladder still up and extended!

Here he is, driving the ladder truck with the big mechanical ladder extended and hanging slightly to one side. The people shopping downtown must have wondered what the hell was going on.

He made it back to the station without hitting a single power line or street sign. As luck would have it, he drove back on the streets that just had all of the power lines buried.

He whipped around the downtown firehouse and started backing in. Right above our apparatus room doors was the mayor's office. The mayor looked up and saw the ladder heading right for his big plate glass window!

Luckily, one of the firefighters on duty saw the chief backing in with the ladder up. But, of course, he also was one of the only guys on the job that stuttered when he got excited.

He ran out of the station waving his arms wildly:

"S . . . s . . . s . . . STOP!"

Old Dad saw him in the side mirror and hit the brakes!

When he got out, he looked at the ladder, extended up about twenty feet in the air, and turned bright red.

He was incredibly flustered! The other firefighters helped put the ladder down. Old Dad backed it into the station and went right to his office.

His phone was ringing off the hook.

It was the mayor.

We never, ever had to use the ladder truck for hanging banners again.

Let's Make a Skydive!

The year was 1980. I had been a firefighter for almost a year and was having the time of my life. A twenty-year-old with a great job running into burning buildings. What could be better?

One day we were all sitting around the coffee table at the downtown firehouse and I mentioned that I always wanted to make a parachute jump, ever since I was a little kid. Some of the other firefighters said they wanted to make a jump too, so it all began right there, at that moment, at the firehouse.

We found the only skydiving center close to us in the phone book (remember those?) and made the call. The drop zone owner said it would be sixty-five dollars for all of the training, the gear, and the jump, per person. That sounded okay to everyone on my shift, so we posted a flyer on the firehouse bulletin board to see if anyone on the other shifts wanted to join us in our death-defying adventure.

Six brave dummies signed up to make the first jump course. We collected the cash up front from each person, so no one had any wiggle room to back out on the big day. We carpooled up to the skydiving center and had some friends tag along just to watch. (Well, they mostly came along to heckle us.)

I'm not sure what I expected a drop zone to look like, but this wasn't it! There was a faded sign at the end of a country road that said "Parachute Center" with an arrow giving the direction. When we pulled in to the parking area it looked like we were at a regular farm but with a grass runway. The office area was in a big old farmhouse and there was a tiny, little Cessna airplane parked out by a metal hangar. Dale, the owner and, unbeknownst to us, one of the most famous jumpers in Ohio, came out to greet us. They were excited a group of firefighters were going to jump with them and had everything ready to go for our course. There were a few other folks that were going to hurl themselves out of this imperfectly good little Cessna on that sunny Saturday afternoon. The peanut gallery that drove up with us to watch couldn't believe we were going to go through with it.

We signed all of the legal "you can't sue us if the parachute doesn't work" paperwork and paid them the collected cash. I guess this was it: we're jumping out of an airplane over a cornfield in Ohio!

The training was intense. Dale walked us out to the hangar. That was going to be our "classroom" for the next couple of hours. He showed us all of the gear, how it worked, what handles did what to which parachute, and pictures of parachutes gone wrong so we would be able to save ourselves with a reserve canopy if needed.

There were hanging harnesses we all had to get into. The harnesses had handles in the right places to simulate the gear, and we had a "belly mount" reserve parachute hooked to us. Dale barked out orders to us while we were dangling from the ceiling.

"Mae West, what do you do"?

"Streamer! Cutaway! Look, Pull, Punch!"

He barked orders at us rapidly, yelling when we got something wrong or out of order. Yup, this was the closest thing to boot camp I had ever seen. And what the hell does the actress Mae West have to do with a parachute anyways?

The moment of truth finally arrived. Dale was satisfied, after a few hours of training, we all might just somehow remember what to do and save our lives on a jump.

Motorcycle helmet: check. Big goggles: check. Belly mount reserve: check. Main parachute: check. Old coveralls for a jumpsuit: check.

The skinny 160-pound kid was ready to jump. We were going to do a static line jump. A long tether attached to the airplane would automatically open the main parachute, which was an old T-10 Army model. Old T-10 canopies were round, not very maneuverable, and not very slowing.

I volunteered to go first. The excitement was building inside of me and I was more scared than ever before.

As I walked to the plane, the heat was relentless from the afternoon sun. The gear felt like a grand piano on my back and the belly mount reserve was pulling me over in the front.

ground and was filled with amazement. I just jumped out of an airplane and lived.

I'm cool, oh yeah!

No time for bragging rights now, however, because that cornfield is rapidly rising up to greet me. Feet and knees together, parachute landing fall, get ready to flare.

Ready, set, WHAM. Ouch! That Ohio soil is pretty tough stuff.

I hit the ground and kicked up a cloud of dirt. I stood up and dusted myself off. I'm alive!

Now the funny part of all of this is we were being filmed for a Pittsburgh kid's morning television show. This really chubby man with crazy hair was the "director." The plan was to shoot all of the footage, and then have the kids do a voice over for their show. After we all made our first jumps, we were ready for beer. But Cecil B. DeMille wanted one more jump out of Kurt, the firefighter they were filming the most for the show. Kurt got back in another parachute rig and went up for his second jump.

Of course, it happened. He broke his ankle on the landing!

I guess he took that Hollywood "break a leg" saying a little too serious. I've recently asked KDKA in Pittsburgh if they have any of the film from the show. It seems all of it was destroyed or lost. That kind of sucks because it would have been great footage of all of us. Except for the broken ankle, we all had a fantastic day!

I went back for a few more jumps that summer and again the next year. I eventually got my skydiving license a few years later and have had more adventures around the globe than I could have ever imagined.

I went back to the Cleveland drop zone years later after I had about a thousand or so skydives and actually got to jump with Bob, his daughter, and a group of local jumpers on one of her milestone skydives. That was really an honor and a fun skydive.

Dale passed away a few years ago, and Bob and his family recently sold the drop zone. The new owners are doing a great job, so if you're ever in the Cleveland, Ohio, area, check out the Cleveland Skydiving Center and make a leap. It might just change your life, like it did mine.

THE DOWNTOWN FIRE OF 1981

I had been on the department a couple of years and was really starting to dislike wintertime. After spending that year in California after high school, I was really missing that nice weather. We were getting some brutal cold fronts and fighting fires in that weather was never much fun. It was a very chilly and snowy evening when my cousin Paula tracked me down at a friend's house.

"You gotta get downtown now, the theater is on fire!"

I could hear the seriousness in her voice, but still thought maybe she just wanted me to come out and meet her and her friends for some drinks. It was a Thursday evening and one of the downtown bars she was calling from was always packed, regardless of the weather.

"Come on Paula, you just want me to come and meet you guys for beers." Just then, I could hear sirens and air horns in the background, as she was calling me from the outside pay phone. I hung up and headed right out.

I arrived at the East Side to get my gear as quick as I could. Most of the turnout gear was gone from the storage area; I knew the department must have called out everyone. As I crested the hill coming into downtown, I could see the glow and the smoke.

An entire city block was on fire!

There was a parking lot right across the street that I managed to get in to. There were car loads of people driving down just to watch the action. I put on my gear and found Old Dad to see what needed to be done. He wanted us to get the ladder truck set up and start pouring some water into the upstairs windows of the building. The front, four story office building that almost took up an entire block was on fire. It had the hallway that lead from the front of the office building to the entrance of the grand old theater. Luckily, there was a firewall and fire doors to keep the fire from devasting the magnificent theater interior. It was built in 1922 and had a grand chandelier, a balcony, and all sorts of underground changing rooms and backstage areas. If the fire penetrated the fire doors and fire walls or jumped from roof to roof, we would have one hell of a battle. The office building housed a few small clerical offices and a giant camera store and photography studio on the entire ground floor. Unfortunately, people were losing wedding, yearbook, and family photos, and there was nothing we could do to save them.

Mutual aid was coming in from surrounding towns. We managed to secure a pumper to get us water to the ladder truck. The fire kept growing, even as we were pouring about

After about an hour or so I looked down—much to my horror! I couldn't see the Night Commander anywhere, but Timmy Coconuts was standing on the turntable, looking at the controls! I tried to shout down to him to not touch anything. I was so frozen; my face couldn't move and nothing was coming out as I tried to yell down. I chopped a tiny piece of ice and threw it down at him to get his attention. Nothing! Just then, to my relief, Steve returned from trying to get us some coffee and yelled at Timmy to not touch anything and get off of the ladder truck. It was comic relief I needed.

I eventually freed the ladder from the building and worked my way back down the aerial ladder. Steve fired it up and we tried to bring it down using the hydraulic controls. There was so much ice still in the guide rails, it wouldn't budge in or out. We could move it away from the building and turn it, but the ladder rails just wouldn't budge, up or down. One of the legendary retired fire captains showed up to see if he could help us. Johnny told us this had happened one other time, and all we had to do was drain out the hydraulic fluid and it would come down under its own weight.

We went to get the chief, because neither one of us wanted to be responsible if we did this and something bad happened. Old Dad came back and discussed it with Johnny. They had worked together for years, and both agreed that we either drain the fluid or leave it until springtime when it would thaw. Johnny helped Steve drain the hydraulics. We just stood there for a few minutes watching to see what would happen. All of a sudden,

BAM!

The first rail collapsed down into the second rail! Ice went flying everywhere, and we all dove for cover.

BAM!

The second rail, along with the first, collapsed down, and more ice chips went flying!

We surveyed the damage. We also saw the look on the chief's face, as he knew this was going to be expensive to get the ladder checked out before we could use it again. We managed to get it working and got it lowered and into the bed secure. I was freezing and needed some dry gloves, so Steve let me drive it back to the station, as that old ladder truck had a good heater.

I warmed up, grabbed some lunch, and headed back over to the scene. We spent the afternoon chopping hose out of the ice and dragging it back to the hose tower in the utility pickup truck.

What a mess. I started thinking about Johnny and Roy from *Emergency!*, fighting fires in sunny California. I wasn't sure I wanted to do twenty years of this snow and ice bullshit!

That evening some of the firefighters were standing under the marquee. The movie that was playing was *Hangar 18*. Old Dad came by and yelled at the guys to get out from under it, as it had a bunch of ice accumulated on the top. I immediately flashed back to when Q Ball had us move away and the chimney crashed down where we were sitting when I was a volunteer.

"Holy shit!" Everyone yelled.

stacked up waiting at the intersection. I passed on the tips of backing in that Red had given me, and it seemed to help.

It was a quiet shift. Nothing was happening in the city, and I was fine with that! Timmy was a nice guy; his wife worked at a local pizza joint a few blocks away and would stop in once in a while on her way to work. He was easy to get along with, I just worried whenever we had a fire. He wasn't in very good shape for a young man, and he would get worn out easily at a fire.

I never liked it when we would get down to just five guys on duty. On this shift we had myself and Timmy at the East Side and the Night Commander, Ray driving for him, and Shmitty as the Houseman. The chief would also respond from home if needed. The only thing that saved us on many occasions was the fact that everyone was required to live in the city. We had twenty-nine members on the job, so you could always call out firefighters from home quickly. And we also had a fire hydrant, with great water pressure, nearly every hundred feet in town. On days like this, we didn't have anyone to drive the ladder truck, and that sometimes was an issue. Usually the first person that arrived at the downtown firehouse on a call out would bring it to the scene.

At about 6 p.m. the fire phone rang. We picked up and listened in as Steve took the info. There was a house on fire down on First Street, the scene of many previous fires that summer.

As we were getting on the rig, the fire phone was ringing off of the hook. We knew that meant that everyone in the neighborhood was seeing it and that we had a real working fire.

Timmy fired up the pumper and started out the narrow bay doors. We slowed down to a stop as he was slipping the clutch to the point I could smell it burning up. What the heck? Finally, we lurched forward and cleared the doors and headed up towards the fire call. As we reached the top of State Street, we could see the smoke, thick and jet black. We had a ripper!

Steve radioed us that they had fire showing out of the upstairs windows! I asked Timmy to slow down a bit. He was getting excited and driving a bit erratic, grinding away at the gears.

We turned on to First Street. There were a lot of residents hanging around and kids on their bicycles in the street watching. This was becoming an almost weekly occurrence on this tree-lined street of older homes, and every fire drew quite the crowd. The downtown crew had arrived a few seconds before us and laid their own supply line, as the hydrant was right next to the house on fire. I hit the siren and air horn hard to get everyone out of our way and eventually made it to the burning house.

Steve yelled to me to take an attack line up the stairs. His helmet was around his neck and hanging off of his head. I could see him looking around.

"Are you looking for your helmet"?

"YES!"

"It's around your neck, you dumbass!"

city workers that brought in and exchanged the big rat traps monthly. There were old Civil Defense boxes of plastic shrink-wrapped dry food, barrels of drinking water, and a lot of old filing cabinets from city hall's years-gone-by records. We were well prepared in case the Russians nuked us!

The boiler was down there, as well as the water heater. In the wintertime, that musty smelling basement made the craziest creaks and popping noises you have ever heard. Whenever someone would turn on a water faucet, pipes would rattle and shake. There was a very steep and narrow stairway that lead down to the dark abyss from the gear storage room. I think in four years of working there, I only went down to that dungeon four or five times.

There were two fire trucks in the station. One was a 1960s-era Mack pumper. That was our frontline unit. The other was a 1940s-era American LaFrance pumper. It was the old type of fire truck with one bench seat and a long nose out in front. It had a giant red bubblegum-machine type red light on the roof and a very loud mechanical siren on the fender. It didn't have power steering and it was slower than molasses. It had to be double clutched on every gear, both shifting up and down, and it had the turning radius of the Queen Mary. What a pain in the ass to drive!

Some of the firefighters rebuilt it and made it into a foam unit equipped with AFFF (a type of foam to coat and smother oil fires). Every once in a while, we would get zinc dust or oil fires at one of the mills, and we would respond with the old LaFrance. Little kids on tricycles could have gotten to a call faster than that thing!

"Hey Timmy, what's up? Are you working here today?" I asked.

"Yeah, Grimmy, the chief sent me here for some driver training shifts with Luke."

Timmy waddled around the firehouse, getting his safety gear on the pumper and checking out the equipment. This was going to be good I figured. Timmy would provide some comic relief for sure; I just didn't realize how much at the time.

The guys worked with Timmy over time to mold him into a better firefighter. It was a slow process. In Timmy's heart, he still wanted to be a cop.

I stuck around for a bit; Timmy seemed worried about something.

"Are you OK, Timmy?"

"Sort of. I saw this really disturbing movie last night, *Poltergeist*."

"Poltergeist?" I asked.

"Yeah, it's about ghosts and stuff. It's really a scary movie."

"Do you like those sorts of scary movies? I don't."

"They'ren't just movies you know; ghosts are real." Timmy exclaimed.

Just by the look on his face I knew he was serious. Here he was, a twenty-eight-year-old man that believed in ghosts. My mind raced, and I couldn't resist.

"Do you know about the ghost of Henry Putt?"

Old Dad couldn't figure out why Timmy called him in a panic, wanting a transfer back downtown. Timmy's brother-in-law was a cop in town. He asked him to patrol the East Side firehouse and watch out for strange things at night. Timmy told all the guys at each shift change about the old pumper starting up in the middle of the night. He even called the city mechanic to see if it was possible for a fire engine to start up all by itself in the middle of the night, asking questions about the battery and magnetos self-igniting the pumper!

Poor Timmy Coconuts would never get much rest and was seriously afraid of old Henry.

The guys couldn't resist: they snuck up a few more times and started it up on him. Each time Timmy was more scared. It was torture for him. Old Dad lived across the street from the East Side. The firefighters were always worried about getting busted by him if they were there in the middle of the night starting up the pumper. That would be hard to explain!

One night they had just started up the pumper and left in the chief's car when Old Dad himself drove by. Old Dad liked his beer and enjoyed going out on the weekends with his wife to polka at a local bar that had great pizza and music. As he drove by on his way home, he saw the revolving red light lit up. He was furious! He called the station at 2 a.m. and chewed some serious butt. Red explained that they were testing out the old pumper that night and must have left the battery on. Quick thinking! In the meantime, Timmy was having another panic attack.

They had started the pumper up on Timmy about four or five times over about six months. Finally, they let it rest for a while as it was really affecting him.

One night, Steve, the Night Commander, decided he wanted to sneak up and start the truck up on Coconuts. It had been a while and Timmy was working with Luke at the East Side. They worked it out that Steve would sneak up and fire up the old yellow pumper about two in the morning. Steve is a giant of a man and would laugh so hard the entire firehouse would shake during a good story! He would beat the walls laughing during a good joke and loved a firehouse prank as much as anyone I've ever known. He was assigned downtown and desperately wanted in on the Henry Putt ghost action.

It was all set up earlier in the shift between Luke and Steve. Steve drove up to the firehouse and parked on the side of the road. It was pitch black out. He snuck up to the firehouse side door. As he opened the door . . .

HOOOOONK!

The air horn on the Mack pumper went off! Steve jumped out of his shoes. Timmy sat straight up in his bed and shouted "Oh, no!"

Luke pulled a double whammy! A real practical-joke coup. Maybe the best of all time.

He had tied a piece of fishing line from the firehouse door knob to the air-horn rope on the Mack pumper. He left the battery on. When the Night Commander slowly and quietly opened the side door, the line pulled down the air horn rope and off it went!

HUGE money compared to the $17,500 per year I was making. I showed the flyer to Old Dad. He couldn't believe firefighters made that much money. I let him know I was giving my two weeks' notice. He was really sad, but also understood. I thanked him for giving me such a great start at the age of nineteen. I knew he had stuck his neck way out for me to get me hired. Especially being an "Ohio kid"!

My dad basically flipped out when I told him I was resigning and heading back to California. I already had four years and four months on the job, and I could retire at 50 percent pay after twenty years. He begged me to stay. But he also understood why I needed to go. The mill my grandfather poured hot steel at for all of those years closed up and all of the worker's pensions and widow's pensions were slashed. It was a terrible situation for everyone in the city. My mom just said go and have fun, you're young and will be fine. And she knew my relatives were there for me if I really needed anything.

I sold everything I had except my Corvette, my hockey gear, and a small bag of clothes. My good friend, and all-around fantastic hockey player, "Howard the Flying Frenchman" agreed to help me drive to California. On a snowy morning on December 3, 1983, Howard and I met the Night Commander for one final breakfast downtown and off westward we motored.

This is in New Mexico with Howard on our way west. We figured it
would be really hot in New Mexico, because cactus grew there, but
what did we know, a couple of Ohioans? There was ice on the roads,
and we were freezing!

When we arrived, Randy was happy to see us and had my
small room ready to move into.

I took the test for Glendale and a number of other
departments. While waiting in line for an application in
Glendale, I met a guy named Aldo, who played hockey at the
old rink where I used to work. We ended up becoming good
friends and played on the same beer league teams.

I took a test for a city that was hiring firefighter inspector/
investigator positions. My uncle Jim owned a music store in
the city, and I managed to meet some of the firefighters there.
I knew this would be a great opportunity as I had met a few
of the officers in the fire prevention bureau, including Chief
Pish, a great guy originally from New Jersey, and Wild Bill,
the fire prevention captain. I did well on the written test and
learned as much as I could about the city and department.
I aced the interview and came out number one on the list! I

don't know how the hell I pulled that one off, but I was offered the job.

I started as a fire prevention inspector/investigator in July 1984 with a six-station suburban department near Los Angeles.

I did it. Life was good!

I had stopped in to the fire prevention office after taking the written test to learn as much as I could about the office before my interview. That helped me tremendously as I must have made a good impression on Chief Pish. He loved that I was a "back East" kid, and I guess I asked all of the right questions. Chief Pish and Wild Bill, the bureau's captain and assistant fire marshal, were two fantastic gentlemen to work for and with, and they had a great effect on my career. I called him Wild Bill because he wore black cowboy boots with his uniform and was a huge fan of Elvis.

It was a huge adjustment for me to now be on a big-time fire department that had more firefighters on duty at the main firehouse than we had every shift in Pennsylvania. The department had a chief, an assistant chief, three battalion chiefs, and Chief Pish, the fire marshal and a training chief. The department also had a paramedic program. They even had a bomb squad, one of the few run by a fire department in the nation at that time.

There was a lot I was going to have to learn!

The fire prevention bureau had Chief Pish, Wild Bill as his assistant fire marshal, three fire prevention inspectors, myself, Bruce and "Stinky," and a couple of civilian inspectors and secretaries. Our office was upstairs in the main firehouse downtown.

It was a great opportunity. I was sent to a myriad of different training courses, including the FBI bomb scene investigation course and the National Fire Academy's Arson and Fire Inspection course in Maryland. I even had to take a course to legally carry a gun, as we were fire investigators and were assigned to a police detective to go out for interviews of arson suspects. It was all head turning stuff for a kid that worked at a two-person firehouse!

After almost two years in fire prevention, a spot opened up on the ladder truck at Station One. I put in for a demotion from fire inspector to firefighter and it was approved. I was missing the action as a firefighter and tiring of the office work. I had arrested a few people for arson and gotten convictions. But that just wasn't as satisfying as running into a burning building. I never cared about the pay, so going from the engineer pay grade to firefighter wasn't an issue. The assignment was on the legendary "C" shift, known for being a rough crowd, and you had better have thick skin to work with that crew. It was a perfect fit for me! They did look at me funny, however, when I would lay some Western Pennsylvania lingo on them: "I'll run the sweeper" or "Yinz guys want some chip chop ham for lunch?" or "Red up the kitchen."

The battalion chief was Larry Doan, one of the calmest and most skilled leaders I've ever had the pleasure of working with. The engine company (pumper) had the Champ, known for winning a huge amount at a blackjack table in Las Vegas once, driven by the engineer known as the Viking due to his massive strength and boating skills, with rookies Rob G Rob and Pike Pole.

Station One "C" shift. Left to right, Chief Doan, the Champ, the Viking, Rob G Rob, Pike Pole, myself, and the Geez. I think this was Pike Pole's twenty-second birthday.

The Truck company had myself and Bobby T. Norm as the engineer and our salty captain we called the Geez. The Geez was also the commander of the department bomb squad. To work at a firehouse with nine people on duty was sure a different setting than what I was used to at the old East Side back in Pennsylvania. However, the antics and the practical jokes were the same. And, we were running a ton of emergency calls—I was loving it!

Truck One with me, Norm, the Geez, and Bobby T, circa 1986.
And, wait for it . . . There was NO SNOW.

My first big fire on Truck One. We were inside with hose lines
a few minutes before this was taken!

CHIEF PISH

The more you screw up, the higher they promote you.

—The Night Commander

Chief Pish was a real character.

I always got along with him great. We would often laugh about the difference in living on the East Coast and being in California. He had grown up Italian as could be in New Jersey and never really left his roots far behind. He loved a good prank and could tell a funny ten-minute story in three hours!

He was about five foot eight with jet black hair combed back neatly. He was always working out and wasn't shy about telling you how many sit ups or pushups he could do at his age. He always reminded me of an older Fonzie, just substitute the leather jacket for a white shirt and gold badge.

Chief Pish worked his way up the ranks. He was a captain, then made it to the chief of the training division, and finally was the city fire marshal.

He ran the department's fire academy and was a very highly respected gentleman in the Southern California fire service. He knew everyone in Southern California's fire service ranks. And nearly everyone knew him personally or had heard some stories. He was a pretty big personality.

Chief Pish was picked to set up a training burn at a deserted giant old wooden hotel up in Lake Arrowhead. This is a great spot in the mountains high above the smog, full of giant pine trees and, of course, the lake.

All of the area fire departments were invited to participate. There were fire crews there from our department, Lake Arrowhead, Big Bear, San Bernardino City, Redlands, Upland, and others. The planning took a few months with the local training gurus, with Chief Pish chosen to lead all of the day's training.

The plan was for one company of firefighters at a time to pull up, lay a supply line, pull the attack hose line, and fight a fire in a room. They would burn one room at a time, so they would have plenty of action for all of the crews. The firefighters on the engine companies (the pumpers) would attack the fire and the truck company crews (the ladder truck) would cut some holes in the roof for ventilation. They were also going to put some mannequins in for search and rescue drills.

In fire department talk, this was basically a training chief's wet dream!

They made a schedule for each unit: what room they would extinguish, what truck companies would ventilate with which

I grabbed Stinky by the shirt and pulled him next to me.

"Shut the hell up and let's get out of here."

Stinky looked at me really confused.

I drug him by his shirt to the door.

Well, what the hell was wrong with me, he asked!

"Stinky, the cops were all over the bank."

"Huh."

Now Stinky wasn't always the most observant guy in the room. One time we had a car fire and he said it was electrical. But the car didn't even have a battery in it! But that's a story for another chapter.

"Stinky, let's come back later."

We went to the small sandwich shop a block away and grabbed some lunch and went back to the office.

About twenty minutes later, in storms Davidson.

"You dumbass!" He was hot.

"We have been watching these bank robbers for two weeks!"

"You just blew my cover and the guys walked out of line right after you did! Those were FBI guys at the manager's desk."

Davidson was now *really* worked up! Stinky turned bright red and started to apologize profusely to Davidson. Detective Davidson stormed out of our office.

I learned my lesson.

Never.

Ever.

Wave to a plainclothes detective at the bank until he waves first!

The bank robbers were caught in a neighboring city a week later. Whew!

I was called into Chief Pish's office the next day. I was put in charge of securing a couple mannequins from the local department store. We were going to do a test at the training center. One was going to be covered with grain alcohol and the other with gasoline. The test was to be filmed. Big shot representatives from Taser were going to be there, along with the police chief and his lieutenants, the fire chief, the city manager, the mayor, and others. I was to document everything, write a report, and edit the video with some narrative. I was to interview the sergeant involved, and it all needed to be done sooner than later.

This was going to be a big deal, as the threat of a giant lawsuit was looming.

On the test day the fire department's training center was packed with observers in suits and uniforms. We doused the mannequins and stood them up out in the large open area.

They shot the grain alcohol one first.

Nothing.

Then, they shot the one covered in gasoline.

WHOOSH! Like Johnny Torch.

The mannequin erupted into a giant ball of flame. The looks on their faces told it all.

Damn.

They all huddled together and discussed it. The police chief asking the Taser guys why there was no warning in the training. The Taser executives were covering their tracks by saying who would be dumb enough to shoot a guy covered in gas with 50,000 volts!

The victim died a week or so later, and the city eventually paid a hefty sum for a wrongful death lawsuit.

There is now a warning label about using a Taser near flammable liquids.

No good deed goes unpunished . . .

The fire should have been going down, but it was growing. The chief was yelling at him to get some water on the fire!

Ricky was giving it all he had. The glow was getting bigger and then finally just went out in an instant. But fire was still blowing out of the front window. He was so confused!

He had been shooting water at the fire through the front door at the seat of the fire just like he had been trained in the fire academy.

Well, of course the fire he was squirting for five minutes went out. It was a giant hall way mirror that finally broke! It was on an entry way closet door and was reflecting the fire in the living room!

He didn't get a drop on the fire.

What a dumbass!

AMNESTY

In 1986, Ronald Reagan pressed congress to pass an amnesty act. It allowed people who were in the country illegally before 1982 to declare amnesty and be able to live and work in the USA legally.

Offices started offering the paperwork to sign up. In the city, it was not uncommon to find an office that cashed paychecks, sold bus tickets to Tijuana, offered car insurance, and provided the amnesty paperwork.

One night at about one o'clock we were called to assist the police department. They needed a ladder to get up on the roof to check for some bad guys. There was a strip mall that had a bar, a pawn shop, and an amnesty office in a row all next to each other. The pawn-shop burglar alarm went off, and the cops wanted to check the roof, as we had been experiencing a rash of business break-ins that were conducted through the roof vents in the downtown area.

We rolled out of bed and fired up the ladder truck, grumbling about why the hell don't the cops buy their own damn ladders! We drove over the couple of blocks to the business and were

A firefighter had transferred out due to a promotion, so we had an open spot to fill. We had heard through the grapevine that some new rookies were hired. I'll never forget the day I met our newest firefighting machine. I walked into the station locker room and there was this tall skinny kid with a little boy haircut. He said hi to me, and I just walked by and nodded. I thought he was some Boy Scout or paramedic trainee ride along.

Nope! He was our new rookie!

I went back into the kitchen and asked the Champ who the little kid was in the locker room.

Everyone just busted out laughing.

"Reaper, that's our twenty-year-old, newest Station One ass-kicking firefighting paramedic!" cackled the Champ.

On day one, the Champ told him he looked like a pike pole, long and skinny, and that was it. The name stuck forever! Pike Pole became my partner in crime around the firehouse. We became fast friends and got into all sorts of shenanigans, and, of course, off duty ones also!

Pike Pole was a fantastic paramedic and firefighter. He recently retired, and over a beer at his retirement dinner we were cracking up about this one:

It always seems lunchtime brought a call or two for us. We had just sat down to eat and the alarm goes off.

"Engine One, report of a trapped person in a house."

What the hell?

For whatever reason, I was riding on Engine One that day. We jumped on the unit and headed to the house in question. The Viking stopped the rig and we hopped off, wondering how someone was trapped in a house. A gardener was there. He said he was the one that called 911, as he had heard cries for help coming from inside the tiny house.

We went up to the front door of the little bungalow. There was a row of them. All studio type places with a bedroom and living room in the front and a very small bathroom and kitchen in the same room.

We heard it. A faint cry...

"Heeeeelllp. Heeellp. I'm stuck . . . heeellp."

I looked at Pike Pole and shrugged. The door was locked, so there was only one thing we could do that we're good at: we bashed open the door.

As we went in the very tiny, little house, the heat and the stench hit us like a ton of bricks. It was a hot summer day, over 100 degrees, and the inside of the house had to be about 130!

There were all sorts of candy wrappers and empty potato-chip bags strewn about the bed. There were piles of newspapers and empty soda cans and bottles all across the floor. Half-eaten Oreo containers and Twinkies were on a chair.

"Help . . . help." The faint voice was coming from the bathroom.

speed. They cut up a car with the extrication tools and had the roof and doors off in minutes. It was a spectacular show, especially with all of the recruits jumping out of the fourth-floor window on to the big round rescue net.

The families were all applauding and beaming with joy.

It was a spectacular display. I was so proud of Aldo. It takes a lot of hard work to make it through a Los Angeles City fire academy.

And then they had one last show.

They had an LAFD helicopter come in to do a display of a long line rescue, where the helicopter would drop a firefighter in, hook up to a patient, then hoist them back up, and fly away.

As the big Bell 412 helicopter (it's sort of a twin-engine Huey) came in to the area, it made a tremendous racket.

Whop, whop, whop as the main rotors chopped the air into submission!

And then the giant helicopter got over the crowd at about fifty feet up . . . and that is when the mayhem started.

All of the chief's dress uniform white hats went flying everywhere! *All* of the women in the stands were holding on to their hair and dresses! It was like a mini hurricane had just hit.

The chiefs were trying to wave off the helicopter.

Dust was flying everywhere.

A guy in the stands lost his toupee!

As the helicopter descended a little lower, the rotor wash and noise got even worse! WHOP! WHOP! WHOP!

The rookies were all scrambling to grab the chief's hats. Women in the stands, with their children, started to run away from the wind and dust. It was mayhem!

The pilot was radioed to get away from the crowd as soon as he could safely and slowly fly away, with the firefighters still dangling from the hoist cable!

It took about twenty minutes for everyone to come back to the stands and for the ceremony of the badge pinning to resume.

A graduation no one will ever forget!

Most rookies have no clue what they're about to encounter during their career. The emergency calls they go on will vary greatly, and the opportunity to make life and death differences appear often during time on the job.

Aldo and his crew were called to the 1988 First Interstate Tower fire in downtown Los Angeles a few years after he was hired. They were inserted by helicopter onto the roof of the sixty-two-story high rise and worked their way down to rescue some trapped citizens. I was on duty at my firehouse and watched it live on the local news. Five floors were totally involved. They worked their way down into the smoke and heat to perform the rescue. I'm sure the thought of a rescue like that never crossed his mind during the academy! Aldo and his crew were awarded for bravery and a job well done by the mayor and city council. Aldo and his wife eventually moved to a fire department in Idaho for a slower lifestyle.

dashboard mounted mic and keyed it. They were broadcasting their entire conversation!

For about fifteen minutes they let every fire truck in four cities know about their sexual prowess with their former girlfriends as "bedpan commandos" on the ambulance! And loudly, as they were shouting to each other over the noise of the truck's diesel engine!

On the gurney in the ambulance!

At the ambulance station!

In their parked car!

They described, in great detail, all of their ambulance-company sexual shenanigans. It was maybe the most X-rated conversation to ever broadcast over the air from a fire truck in the history of the fire service! The dispatchers were desperately trying to contact them. However, when you're broadcasting, you can't receive!

Firefighters out in the cities were hearing every single word and knew exactly who it was talking. They couldn't believe it! As the two lover boys pulled around the corner into the back of the training center, there was Chief Snidely, waving his arms wildly and pointing to his hand-held radio like a mad man!

"What the hell does that idiot want?" one of them blurted out. Well, you can only imagine the ass chewing they received from Snidely Whiplash after they parked.

But like my wise old East Side-firefighter pal Steve told me, we all have more ass than the chiefs have teeth!

Ropes and Knots

The less time you spend in an intersection, the less time
there is for an idiot to hit you.

—The Viking

It's hard work to be a rookie on the fire department. You have to be in constant motion. You're the first to arrive in the morning and make the coffee, put the flags up, and grab the newspaper from the front apron of the station and bring it into the kitchen, hoping like hell it didn't get rained on or wet from the lawn sprinklers. You have to study for written tests and manipulative tests. Lots of them! One of test is on tying knots.

I was working with my usual crew on Truck One downtown. The Geez was our captain. He had been on the job since they had horses and dalmatians. He was also the commander of our bomb squad. Norm had also been on forever. He was our engineer, responsible for driving the unit and keeping all of the equipment, such as chain saws, up to speed. I was the senior firefighter, and we had Scotty with us this shift. A brand-new rookie.

Scotty wasn't exactly brand new. He had worked a few years already for another department. He was a down to earth guy. Pretty strong and always a wad of chew in his mouth. Scotty not only had to prove himself as a rookie with us but he had GIANT shoes to fill. His dad, Bill, worked at our department for years. Bill was legendary, and the stories about him were fantastic. He was one of the strongest guys to ever work on the job. He was a fearless firefighter that everyone liked and unquestioningly followed into burning buildings. He left our department to be a fire chief elsewhere. Unfortunately, he was diagnosed with cancer and passed away shortly thereafter. All the old-timers on the job knew Bill and had known Scotty since he was born, so he had a big legacy to live up to.

Scotty had been doing a great job. The only trouble he had really gotten into was one shift when he was on the way to a fire call. Engine One was an old open-cab Crown pumper.

Scotty always had a wad of chew and a spit can with him. On the way to the call, as he was putting on his turnout jacket, he knocked the spittle can all over the captain's back! Other than that, he was acing his probationary skill testing, as we all knew he would.

Engine One that day were the usual characters: the Champ; the Viking, one of my best friends and favorite guy to get riled up on the job, and probably the strongest guy to ever work with us; Pike Pole, my partner in crime at the station; and Rob G Rob, paramedic extraordinaire.

The engine and truck shared the firehouse with a battalion chief. However, we also had the headquarter offices of the fire chief, assistant chief, training chief, medic captain, and secretaries with us. We were always getting called to run errands or clean up something or to move desks and filing cabinets around.

We did the morning firehouse clean up and checked out all of the equipment. The Geez went down to the bomb squad office in the basement and just told us to "train with the new kid." Scotty said he didn't need any help and was going to just work on his knots. On the truck company we carry a couple of big red canvas bags. They have a hundred feet of utility rope in them. Scotty drug a couple out of the compartment and started tying away.

"Truck One firefighters to the executive secretary's office please" boomed over the station's PA system. I was out back washing one of the chief's cars with Pike Pole. I walked by and grabbed Scotty, who had a few rope bags out behind the rigs. One of the secretaries that always helped me with my various shenanigans (more on that later) needed some filing cabinets moved. No problem, we're on it! We got the hand truck out of the back storage room and went to work. While we were there moving her filing cabinets, Engine One was dispatched on a medical aid call.

The Viking pulled out of the station, code three (red lights and siren) and rolled toward downtown, He made the turn to head south to the address of the emergency about a half a mile away. They pulled up on scene, the private ambulance company was already there. It was nothing serious; the ambulance could handle it, so the crew jumped back on the rig to head back to the station.

Dispatch called them over the radio. "Engine One, report back to the scene of your accident." They all looked at each other confused. "What accident?" the captain asked over the radio.

"Engine One, you were involved in an accident at Holt and Euclid, please meet the police and the battalion chief there immediately."

"What the hell is going on!" The captain was confused.

"Did we hit something on the way here?"

They were completely perplexed. The firefighters ride the pumper facing backward, and this was *way* back when we had open cabs on the fire trucks—they saw nothing happen out of the ordinary.

Engine One drove back to the intersection of the alleged crash. There was a brand spanking new, very shiny Audi parked by the curb. The lady driving it was quite shaken. The police officers and the battalion chief were taking pictures and getting her statement.

Well. As Engine One went screaming by her on the way to the call, something ripped her entire muffler and exhaust system right off!

Just then, one of the police cars showed up. The officer went to his backseat and pulled out a mangled muffler and exhaust pipe. Then went to his trunk and pulled out 100 feet of rope attached to the red canvas bag with "Truck One" stenciled on it!

Scotty had been tying knots onto Engine One's back handles on the tailboard. He left the rope bag sitting on the tailboard (the back step of the pumper). When we were called into the secretary's office to move filing cabinets, he forgot all about it! When the call came in, the engine company rolled out of the station with the bag sitting there tied to the back handle. The bag of rope fell off on the way! So here they were, driving red lights and sirens to a call, trailing a hundred feet of rope with a big canvas bag attached to it. When they went around the corner, the bag "cracked the whip" and snapped right under the Audi.

WHACK!

It must have been a horrendous noise as it ripped everything off in a split second! Now, not only are they driving up the street, making lots of noise with the air horn and siren, but they're also towing an entire exhaust system behind them with the muffler dancing around. I think Scotty had tied a clove hitch, as it finally worked itself free and the rope came off, dropping everything in the middle of the main street in town!

Word got back to us and Scotty was sweating bullets. I asked him if he was tying things to the pumper.

Yup! Holy Crap!

The battalion chief came back and Engine One soon after. I think the Viking asked Scotty if the rope bag was his and tossed it at him. Everyone was worried. I was supposed to be watching Scotty's training. He worked for the Geez, and the

Viking should have checked his rig before pulling out of the station, according to our standard operating procedures.

"Damn it Scotty, you're gonna get all of us in the barrel!"

And . . . wait for it . . . the PA system blared out loudly across the apparatus room, "Truck One firefighters to the chief's office immediately."

I figured I had a big ass chewing coming at the least, and maybe a written reprimand at the most. Hell, I was more afraid of what the Viking was going to do to us than the chiefs!

However, Scotty might be in serious peril, being that he was a rookie on probation.

He was really upset of course and felt like crap with what had happened.

"Just tell the truth and it will be all OK." I reassured him.

We got to the battalion chief's office and I was told I wasn't needed.

Oh damn! I hope his old department will take him back, I wondered. After about a half an hour he came out, white as a sheet. Luckily, we worked under one of the greatest battalion chiefs in the history of the department, Larry Doan. He realized it was an honest mistake. I can't remember, but I think they just gave Scotty a verbal reprimand as a slap on the wrist. We were all lucky that day. That thing could have wrapped some people walking down the sidewalk or something!

Scotty is a captain now and never ever lets a rookie tie anything to the rig, ever. And, he hung up the chew.

Captain Pick 'N' Flick

In August of 1988 our department was growing and we hired twenty-eight new recruits. We were opening a seventh firehouse that was going to protect the east side of the city with a pumper, a ladder truck, and a second battalion chief. A lot of firefighters were getting promoted and shuffled around; however, we managed to keep most of our crew together at the downtown station.

Every couple of months the recruits were to be moved to different stations. This gave them an opportunity to get to know the different equipment and the layout of the city, with its different hazards and calls. It also gave them a chance to be evaluated by different crews. Like every fire department, some stations were much busier than others.

One day at our station a visiting captain that not many people liked wanted us to move a big conference table. It's a long story, so I'll spare you the details; however, the Viking got me in trouble with him.

About a week later I got my marching papers to go down to Station Two, a three-person pumper in the "barrio" section of the city. The firefighter on this shift was promoted, and I was going to fill in for six months.

Not only was I changing shifts, but I was going to work with a captain everyone called Pick 'N' Flick. Now you can only imagine how he got this nickname. And just for the record, no one in the history of the fire service has ever gotten a nickname they didn't deserve.

I worked my last shift at Station One on the truck company and packed up all my stuff and headed down to my new firehouse. I had heard all of the Pick 'N' Flick stories, but I couldn't believe they were true. I had never ever worked a shift with him.

Luckily, the engineer (the rank of the firefighter that drives the pumper) was as great of a guy as Pick 'N' Flick was a pain in the ass. Sam had an even temperament and somehow was the only person on the entire department that could keep Pick 'N' Flick in line and put up with him. Sam loved traveling, and his stories and travel magazines helped keep me sane those six months.

After working a few shifts with these guys, I could see what everyone was talking about. You couldn't get away from Captain Pick 'N' Flick, as he loved to talk and would follow you to the bathroom door, yakking away!

And then I saw it one evening. The famed move. He picked and flicked, as he watched TV!

Pick 'N' Flick loved watching *Jeopardy* and would sometimes argue with the TV that Alex Trebek was wrong. A twenty-four-hour shift with this guy was like being under some sort of ancient Chinese torture. I was used to having eight other guys around each shift. We would always be playing basketball or volley ball at night, and we always cooked dinner together as a crew. In the evenings I would sit and have coffee with our battalion chief after a game of cards for dishes duty.

This place was like being in solitary confinement.

We ran a *lot* of calls out of Station Two, but firehouse life around the station was just weird because of the captain. Sam would often quietly guide him into good decisions at emergencies.

Sam teamed up with me to cook dinners together. Pick 'N' Flick never wanted to buy in to our meals and would fend for himself.

One late afternoon we received a fire call:

"Engine One, Engine Two, Engine Five, Truck One, Battalion Chief One, structure fire, multiple calls received at 1052 D Street."

Sam opened the firehouse apparatus door and we hopped on the pumper. As we turned out of the station, we heard the battalion chief say on the radio that there was heavy smoke showing.

We knew we had a pretty good fire going. Sam sped up just a little bit.

There was quite a bit of afternoon traffic as usual. When we got to the corner of a major intersection, there were all sorts of cars trying to get out of our way.

As a firefighter, I rode backward in the jump seat, getting all of my protective gear on and donning my breathing apparatus so I would be ready to go when we pulled up at the scene.

We came to a stop and Sam was hitting the airhorn and siren hard!

HOOOONK!

HOOOOOOOOOOONK!

All of us had headsets to cancel out the noise of the siren and air horn and allow us to talk to each other. You can also hear the department radio through the headphones.

"Engine One is on scene, we have heavy smoke and fire out of the upstairs windows, and we're laying a supply line"

HOOOOOOOOOOOOONK!

We're still at a dead stop and Sam blurts out . . .

"That fucking stupid bitch won't get the fuck over and out of our way!"

HOOOOOOOOOOOOOOOOOOONK!

The lady finally pulls out of the intersection and off we go.

A moment of silence and then . . .

Pick 'N' Flick said, "Sam that was my wife"

Bwahahaha! I died laughing!

Pick 'N' Flick's wife, who was an incredibly sweet woman, was bringing him dinner.

It was now complete silence all the way to the call. I had to take my headset off because I was laughing so hard.

We got to the fire scene and got in on the action. We made quick work of it, but the overhaul and hose rolling and hand-tool clean up took a while.

When we returned to the firehouse, there was a plate of food with foil wrapped over it.

I couldn't resist.

"Hey Cap!"

"What!" He was still pissed off.

"You can buy in with us for dinner next shift if you want."

THE MIDDAY MOVING COMPANY

I've been friends with Randy since 1978. We met at our job at Best Products, and became roomies when he invited me out and I moved back to California in 1983.

Circa 1984, Randy had great shorts and I've no idea
how to play a guitar!

We shared Randy's condo in Upland. It was a great place for a couple single guys, as the old El Gato Gordo restaurant and night club was just over the wall behind our development. It was a short stumble home after the Friday afternoon happy hours.

Randy auditioned for and got selected to be on the game show *Concentration*. He beat the hell out of all of the contestants and was buddy-buddy with host, Alex Trebek, by the end of the week! He won a *ton* of prizes, including fabulous vacations and home furnishings. He really crushed it on each episode.

After his amazing weeklong run on the show, we ended up with an entire garage full of merchandise! Refrigerators, washing machines, couches, and end tables. Our garage looked like a home furnishing warehouse.

Randy started dating a girl named Jean. She was this feisty Italian school teacher from Boston. Jean had an apartment in Costa Mesa. She owned some really old looking furniture, so Randy took down our condo furniture that was pretty nice, and we used the new game show swag to replace it at our house. Her place looked a lot better with our old stuff in there, and Randy took her furniture and stored it in our garage.

Over the course of a year or so of dating, Randy grew tired of her act and they broke up. She loved to argue and caused all sorts of havoc every time they would go somewhere. She had a fiery temper and wasn't afraid to release it on a moment's notice! He asked for our furniture back, and, of course, she wasn't having any of that. She said it was hers now.

Randy asked me what he should do. I asked him if he still had a key to her place. He did! Problem solved.

On a gorgeous summer day, we rounded up our pal Doug, who had a work trailer and pickup truck, and used my pickup truck. We loaded up her old crappy furniture out of our garage

Bodine went to the pumper, climbed into the jump seat (the backward facing seat behind the driver) and covered himself with his turnout coat to shield himself from the rain.

The captain and engineer jumped in the cab and looked back, and saw him there and headed back to the firehouse.

When they pulled in to the station and parked, off jumps Bodine. He looked around really puzzled.

"What the heck, where am I?" he asked.

"What the hell are you doing on our rig, you dummy!" the captain blurted. "And where the hell is our firefighter?"

"Who are you and where am I?" Bodine asked, completely confused as to what was happening.

Well, the neighboring city's rig, which looked a lot like Bodine's pumper he was assigned to, was parked close to his. When his captain told Bodine to get on the rig, he accidentally jumped on their pumper and rode back to their main firehouse!

Their firefighter had gone to the hospital in the ambulance, but his captain didn't know it, and when they looked back and saw a person covered in his jacket, they thought it was their own firefighter.

When Bodine's crew got on their rig, they were missing a person, but assumed he had followed up at the hospital and they went back to their firehouse.

So now the rookie is stuck at a firehouse, in another city, about five miles from his station. While on probation.

The captain told him not to worry, no one would ever know about this.

Sure, they won't . . .

He called Bodine's captain and they figured out how this happened. It seemed there were a few confusing orders for which firefighter on scene was going to go to the hospital with which patient.

The ambulance dropped off a firefighter at the station Bodine was at and gave him a ride back to his own firehouse.

He got quite an ass chewing from his captain when he finally got back to his own station.

What a dumbass!

The pan of oil the tortillas were in was on fire! It was spreading to the kitchen cabinets!

"Get an extinguisher off of the pumper. QUICK!"

The entire firehouse was now filling with smoke! The flames were lapping at the overhead kitchen cabinets and running along the bottom to melt the lights over the stove! They had to get low and crawl into the kitchen and blast the pan with a dry chemical extinguisher. The firehouse kitchen smoke detector was blaring.

Joey grabbed some big kitchen mitts and got the burned-up pan outside. The fire had started the cabinets on fire, so they had to check to make sure that was completely put out. They also had to check the exhaust vent over the stove. Some of the grease up there was on fire! They shot some dry chem up and got it put out.

What a mess! But now what?

They for sure didn't want their asses chewed by the battalion chief and for sure didn't want the humiliating story to get around to the other stations, so . . .

They grabbed a big smoke ejector to rid the station of all the smoke. Then they jumped in the rig and went to the hardware store for new supplies to clean up the cabinets and replace the under-cabinet lighting. After working all evening, they had the cabinets and stove looking like nothing had happened. A few gallons of air freshener was sprayed throughout the station!

At shift change some of the oncoming crew said they smelled smoke.

"We burned a few tortillas last night, sorry, but we left you some fish for tacos, enjoy."

Food, it always distracts a firefighter!

The oncoming shift just went along with their morning business. To this day, it was one of the greatest cover-ups in department history!

Shhhhh . . . . .

I went to Station Three after Wayne was transferred. Here left to right, Joey, myself, Bhagwan, and Hop. Circa 1991.

Another activity I had always wanted to do was fly helicopters. When I was thirteen years old, my family took big trip out to California to visit my relatives, towing the trailer my mom eventually blew up. When I begged my dad for a helicopter ride at Mount Rushmore, and we had a wonderful experience, who knew that feeling would eat at me for so long? Our flight was in an old Bell 47 model, the helicopter with the big-bubble cockpit. I always thought about learning to fly, but really didn't know how to go about doing it or where to even go to learn. I looked in the phone book, which seems so archaic now, and found a couple of flight schools close to me. I called a few schools to receive as much info as I could about the costs, the time involved to be licensed, and what helicopters I would be eligible to fly. I took lots of notes but didn't really think I could afford it. I was blowing through my paychecks jumping out of perfectly good airplanes!

The following year I bought a condo at the beach and had this thing called "write-offs" for my taxes. I didn't know a damn thing how all of that mysterious tax stuff worked, and never changed my withholdings. I hired a tax accountant for the first time ever and learned so much about what to do and not do financially. I received a refund of about $4,000. Big money for 1991!

Helicopter lessons, here I come!

In the mid '90s I was flying nearly every week. Helicopters just have a way of being addictive. Very addictive!

I was flying out of a company at Long Beach Airport. The owners became friends of mine, and they gave me a key to the office. I could come in any time and use a two-seat Robinson R22 and go flying around Southern California.

I used to fly out to the drop zone on the weekends. It sure beat the traffic, and I would always end up giving a few rides to my skydiving friends.

I quickly built up enough hours to take my commercial-license check ride. It went pretty smooth, and I was on to maybe a career change. To get a real job in the industry I knew I had to learn how to fly turbine powered helicopters. I kept thinking back to Aldo's graduation and how I would love to fly for one of the large fire departments like Los Angeles City that operate a fleet of water dropping and emergency transport helicopters. The next step was to take a turbine transition course.

I trained to fly turbine helicopters with Masao, a Japanese pilot that was working for a different flight school at the airport. He was the only instructor for the Bell Jet Ranger helicopter that a couple flight schools used for training and scenic flights. Masao was an excellent instructor. I really enjoyed flying with him; however, his English had a very thick Japanese accent, and sometimes he was hard to understand if he became excited.

Ground school covered all of the systems on the helicopter. We spent a weekend learning all about turbine engines, start up and shut down procedures, and emergency procedures and studying the Jet Ranger's operating handbook. Turbine helicopters have a jet type engine, as compared to the Robinson

We flew for about an hour.

He loved it and actually flew pretty well!

Twenty years after our first flight at Mount Rushmore together, I got to take him up for a flight.

We didn't see any seagulls.

It was a great day.

THE LA BLAZERS

Shoot! Shoot! Shoot! And score more goals than they do!

—Coach Art Brewster

I was playing a lot of hockey when I moved back to California. The West Covina rink had a great beer league that was very well run and I skated with a senior A team that had some great talent and a lot of goons. We would play in front of roller-derby type crowds! Some of the games were right out of the movie classic *Slap Shot*.

Just after I was hired, I ran into a firefighter at the rink wearing an "LA COUNTY FD" jersey. I asked him if there was some sort of firefighter team. He gave me the name and number of a firefighter with the Pomona FD. He said they held tryouts and played in the firefighter Olympics once a year against the San Francisco Bay Area firefighter team.

The California Firefighter Olympics are huge. There are participants in many sports from all over the state. There's a

One year in SoCal, we had the legendary Los Angeles Kings announcer Bob Miller be the master of ceremonies, and Kings players Jimmy Fox and Jay Wells guest refereed. After the first period of their first game refereeing, they both came into our locker room. "You guys are freaking crazy!" They couldn't believe how physical a "charity" game was.

We played full-contact NHL rules. There were some broken arms and collar bones and lots of stiches over the years! During the day, firefighters from across the state would be playing softball and basketball or participating in any of the many other sports offered. The participants couldn't wait to come to the hockey games. It was a huge rivalry. Our supporters would drag coolers of beer into the rinks, and sometimes it was so packed with fans, it got hot and the ice started getting watery! A few skirmishes even broke out in the stands over the years between the spectators.

It truly was mayhem. But wow, we sure raised a lot of money!

Art Brewster somehow became our coach through some friends he knew at the rink that had helped us with some skating drills. Art was a real character. He was short, squat, and seemed to know everyone in the National Hockey League. He was a hell of a pencil sketch artist and would draw amazing likenesses of NHL players. Art would help out the Los Angeles Kings by picking up new players at LAX that were traded to the Kings.

One evening at the Kings former home, the old Fabulous Forum, Art was at ice level where he always watched the games from in the corner. One of our Blazer players, Jackie, saw him and managed to get down to say hi and see if he could get Art a beer. As Jackie, who was a boxer in his younger days and is now a famous boxing referee, was talking to Art, someone elbowed Art in the back of the head! Art didn't even look up and just said . . .

"Hi, Gordie!"

Jackie was ready to throw some blows at whoever smacked Art and couldn't believe it. Walking away was Mr. Hockey himself, Gordie Howe, laughing away!

"Nice to see you Art, see you at the Forum Club after the game."

Art knew everyone!

We presented Art (here with his wife) with a Blazers jacket at a team BBQ. It was like giving him a million dollars—he never took it off!

The LA Blazers were now doing well in the tournaments and we actually won the gold medal a couple of times. We packed our gear bags and trekked to Prince George, BC, for a charity game, and some of us went to Chicago for the final game ever at Black Hawk Stadium and skated with our friends there. We would often run into the FDNY players in the Toronto tournament.

With our friends from Prince George, British Columbia

I invited the FDNY to California to play us in a charity game at the big new arena they built in our city. That series became really popular and it has carried on since I retired. I even had the honor of skating for them a few times when they didn't have enough players able to make the trip. When I think of all the amazing firefighters, men and women, I've met through our hockey team, it boggles my mind! One of the people that made a big impact on me was Chief Ray Downey of the FDNY. He played in our Las Vegas tournaments and at that time was a captain on one of the five rescue companies. He always invited me to come to New York City and ride along with him. He was one of the most decorated firefighters in FDNY history. I regret not taking him up on his offer. He was tragically killed on September 11 at the World Trade Center. I'm honored to have known him, and I'm honored to give a huge portion of the proceeds of this book to the Ray Pfeiffer Foundation. I always have a great time when I'm around the FDNY team. All are terrific hockey players and real characters.

It was an amazing invitation for our team. We were asked to play the LA Kings alumni in a charity game. I lined up against Hall of Famer Luc Robitaille on the opening faceoff. Luc has known some of us since his playing days from different benefit events. I asked him if I should check Marty McSorley's curve on his stick. Luc just laughed and said I would do that to my own demise, charity game or not! You can google what happened to McSorley in the 1993 Kings Stanley Cup finals against Montreal if you're not catching on.

On the opening faceoff, one of our fastest skaters, Justin, flew by their entire team and ripped a slapshot over the goalie's glove. His speed and skill caught them off guard, as they weren't used to playing a team of our caliber. Marty McSorley acted very impressed and wanted a photo with Justin. He said no one had ever scored the first goal against them, and he wanted to get a photo with this firefighting hockey phenom! As they all lined up along the bench with Justin, McSorley grabbed a shaving cream pie Mark Hardy had quickly made on a paper plate in their locker room. Justin was grinning from ear to ear while the legendary defenseman, Ian Turnbull, was fidgeting with the camera, allowing time to get the pie delivered to the bench.

Splat! Right in the kisser! The crowd loved it.

Justin turned red and knew he had been had by the best.

move, I push the puck forward until the defender reaches for it, then pull it way back, and then in between my legs, kicking it up to my stick, while holding off the opposing player with my free hand. I would practice this often, and it was my go-to maneuver at least once a game, often to the heckling of my teammates that gave it the name!

Gordie must be wondering how I pulled the famed
"French Pastry" move on him!

I dug the puck out of the net and flipped it up to him. "Hey old-timer, you looking for this?"

He just laughed and said, "That was a pretty slick move, kid."

The very next rush down the ice he skated right for me, puck on his stick. He pushed the puck toward me and then brought it back, passed it through my skates, and took one quick step around me, grabbed it and took a wrist shot from the blue line that went over the goalie's shoulder and off of the crossbar and in! He dug the puck out of the net and flipped it to me,

"Look'n for this, kid?" he said with a big grin on his rugged face.

I was in heaven! Gordie FREAKING Howe just torched me for a goal.

After three hours of playing, our session came to an end, but the day only got better. Gordie had to skate another session in the afternoon and was hungry. We went to the coffee shop next to the rink. It was packed as usual for a Sunday morning. Not one single person recognized him; he liked it that way.

He ordered soup and coffee. We sat there in our corner booth for a couple of hours and listened to Mr. Hockey talk about everything. You could tell he loved Wayne Gretzky like a fourth son and told a great story about number 99 feeding the fishes on a deep-sea fishing excursion with his hockey playing sons, Mark and Marty. He asked each of us what we did for a living. He asked how we all started playing hockey. Gordie talked about his wife, Colleen; sons Mark, Marty, and Murray; and his daughter, Cathy. You could tell how much he loved his family and was so proud of his children. Then he told us a few hilarious NHL stories from way back in the day.

I watched him closely while he sipped his soup. He had a facial twitch, that was noticeable. I'm not sure, but it might have been a result of his horrific skull fracture in the 1950 Stanley Cup playoffs. He was still very muscular, with a tremendously firm handshake. His face was a road map of stiches. I would have loved to ask him about each scar. I'm sure there was quite a story to each and every one of the over

Getting ready for a pregame award

Halfway through the period a giant bench-clearing brawl broke out! The teams were setting the tone for the playoffs in a big way. There were about five players from each team in the penalty boxes. We were watching from ice level, by the Zamboni doors. It was mayhem on every single shift. Both teams were more concerned with throwing their weight around than scoring goals. With about four minutes left in the first period, another giant bench-clearing brawl broke out. It took the referee and linesmen about fifteen minutes to get order restored and put the offenders in the sin bin. The fans were going crazy, and every single person in the arena was on their feet. The coaches and players were losing it, screaming at the officials and each other. The referee went to each bench to calm down the coaching staffs. He stopped the period and made the teams go to their dressing rooms and would add on the time when they came out for period two. It was a really wise move!

We already had our skates on and put on our big costume heads. We stepped on to the ice to cheers from the fans. As we skated around, the announcer introduced the fire chiefs and Smokey and Sparky. The kids were running down to ice level to get a closer look at us. They rolled out a red carpet for the chiefs to accept the check from one of the team's front-office staff.

The crowd cheered, and we skated around again for one final lap to wave at the crowd. Just then Kingston came up and checked into Doak. I couldn't let that happen to Smokey the Bear, so I quickly skated over and Sparky gave Kingston an elbow to the back of his giant furry head.

The crowd loved it!

As Kingston skated away, I looked at Doak and we both had the same idea. We skated down Kingston, dropped our sticks and gloves and started fake punching him to the ice.

The fans went crazy! The kids in the crowd were beating on the plexiglass. We helped Kingston up, grabbed our sticks and hockey gloves, and headed off the ice to a roar of approval. The Zamboni driver was laughing his ass off as he swerved to miss us.

I figured someone from the Kings, or the fire chiefs would be a little upset with our show. Nope! They loved it.

The next day in the Los Angeles Times sports section, there was a big write up about the game. The last sentence read, "The game was so heated, even Smokey the Bear and Sparky the Fire Dog beat up the Kings mascot to the delight of the fans."

as eventually I went out and bought a 46′ Canoe Cove twin-diesel powered boat that I lived aboard in Huntington Harbor for a few years.

We all decided to go diving off of Laguna Beach for lobster and some spear fishing. We loaded up Bailey's boat and the Viking's Sea Ray and met at the Dana Point launch ramp. A couple of guys that didn't dive came along just to fish and drink beer. Jethro Bodine and Ratchetjaw, an older firefighter that could really talk, came along for the fishing and cold ones. Now, I love to tell a good story, but Ratchetjaw could get in twelve stories before I could get halfway through one. He was a tremendously nice guy, but never stopped telling a story to anyone that would listen.

We launched the boats and motored up to Laguna. It was a warm summer day and the sea was very calm and flat, perfect for diving and great visibility.

Finding a nice spot in about thirty feet of water offshore, we anchored within shouting distance of each other. We donned our scuba gear and jumped in, to grab the tasty cockroaches of the sea.

Bodine and Ratchetjaw weren't divers, so they sat up top, guarding our boats with a few cases of ice-cold beer. Ratchetjaw tossed a line over and was trying to catch some fish. All the while yakking away at Bodine.

Non.

Stop.

Yakking away!

After swimming around for almost an hour, I was getting a little low on air and had a game bag full of tastiness. As I was swimming back to the boat about twenty feet down, I saw something flash. It was the lure on Ratchetjaw's fishing line.

I grabbed the line and wrapped it around my hand.

I started swimming as fast as I could down and away from the boat.

"I got one. I got one. It's huge!" Ratchetjaw was screeching with delight!

He was really reeling me in! I had to kick like crazy.

I swam as hard as I could. I would turn and head quickly towards the boat and then swim away, trying to mimic a caught fish. Ratchetjaw was ecstatic!

Finally, I got tired and was almost out of air, and the fishing line was cutting into my dive glove. I grabbed my knife and cut the line.

I waited a few minutes, laughing underwater. I couldn't wait to hear the story.

I returned to the boat about the same time a couple of the other divers were getting back. We took off our fins and got back on board.

Ratchetjaw was going crazy. He really idolized Bailey, who had been his captain at one point, and couldn't wait to tell him about the biggest fish ever he almost caught!

According to Ratchetjaw, he had hooked up the shark from Jaws, whale from Moby Dick, and Shamu from SeaWorld.

Three

It started simple enough.

The plan was for me Horrible, Hessy, and Alger to meet Joey, Chuck and the Viking out at San Clemente Island.

I bought the Mad Divers boat to live on at the marina in Huntington Beach. It was a fun lifestyle, and we would often go out to catch lobster and come back to a giant feast. And I always had fuel to cook them.

The Mad Divers

The Mad Divers was big, twin diesel, and had all of the amenities you could ask for. We had a giant BBQ grill, microwave, TV, water maker, ice maker, fridge, and two nice showers. It was a wonderful floating home.

Horrible and the Viking loaned me a few dollars to buy the Mad
Divers. We had that boat in fantastic shape for fishing and diving.

We were going to leave from my berth in Huntington
Harbor, and Joey was bringing his new big boat he recently
bought, a 42′ yacht fisher, from his berth in downtown San
Diego. We planned on meeting at Seal Cove. Yes, *that* Seal
Cove of cold, uncooked lobster fame!

We provisioned my boat with plenty of beer, some steaks,
and tortillas—and lots of rum and Coke. We shoved off in the
morning and motored out towards San Clemente Island. I
double-checked to make sure there was plenty of propane for
the BBQ grill so we didn't have another tragic lobster episode!

As we got further from the mainland, the sea really started
to get angry. The swells were getting bigger and bigger the
closer we got to San Clemente Island. As we slowly motored
between Catalina Island and San Clemente Island, the seas
now were huge! We were towing Horrible's 14′ Boston Whaler
behind us. I was getting really sea sick, which usually never

I Know We're the Fire Department

O ur new fire chief, Big Fred, flew out to visit a manufacturer that was building a new pumper. They were developing a new rear engine fire truck that would allow for a quieter and roomier cab. He ended up ordering two of them without any of us knowing anything about their specifications. When they arrived, a few of us didn't really like them. The hose bed was a pain to load because of the rear mounted engine and they seemed to always run hot.

And in Southern California summers, they would really run hot.

One day the Engine Seven crew was coming back from a call. A man pulled up next to them and started honking and waving his arms. The engineer that day was the Bhagwan. He looked over to see what was going on with this guy. He was leaning over and shouting . . .

"Your truck is on fire!"

Bhagwan yelled back.

"Yes, we're the fire department."

"NO, YOUR TRUCK IS ON FIRE!"

"Yes, we're going back to the fire station," Bhagwan didn't hear too well.

"YOU'RE ON FIRE!"

The firefighter in the cab finally realized what the driver was shouting.

"Hey Cap, I think we're on fire, Cap!"

Just then the diesel engine sputtered and shut off.

They jumped out of the cab and ran to the back of the pumper. Thick black smoke and flames were pouring out of the engine compartment. They grabbed an extinguisher from a compartment and put it out quickly. Right in the middle of a busy intersection.

How embarrassing!

The score was one pumper burned up and one firehouse kitchen wrecked for the Bhagwan.

To put it mildly, they were all tired of his shit.

Well, it finally happened! It was a Saturday evening and he tuned in to the lottery show, tickets in hand: 6-13-27-1-14-41 and the bonus number of 7.

"Holy *shit!*" he screamed. "I won, I won, I won, *finally.*"

The captain danced around the station. The crew members all wanted to see the ticket, as they all didn't believe him. It was an unreal scene, as the lottery that night was over $300 million pure, green, George Washingtons!

He couldn't control himself: he told everyone to "fuck off! I'm outta here, you losers!"

He stormed into the battalion chief's office. "Here's my badge, Chief, I quit this place!"

He had a few choice words to say about the chief and how he ran the show on his shift too.

Well . . .

Bad move, dude.

Firefighters are the greatest pranksters to ever walk the earth.

His crew had videotaped on VHS a lottery drawing from a few months previous. They went out and bought a quick pick ticket, but added in the winning numbers from the previous show. They put the ticket in the captain's stack he had just played.

They called him to the apparatus floor to check on some bogus issue they made up with the rig to give the crew time to set up the TV. They hit play on the VCR just as the captain came running in to the TV room for the nightly drawing.

Well, after all the excitement cleared and he was calling his wife, they asked him to come in and show him something before he spoke with her.

He stood there in disbelief. He was totally stunned.

After he got done screaming and threatening everyone on his shift with lawsuits, while they were all doubled over laughing, the battalion chief came in.

"Hey, Cap, maybe this firehouse isn't for you anymore and you should consider transferring to a slower station, more time to play the lottery and check tickets, you know."

The chief tossed his badge back to him.

He put in for a new firehouse and was transferred a few shifts later.

because Rob worked at the House of Pain, Station Five—the busiest firehouse in the city. Knowing I had to get my feet wet sometime, I agreed and showed up at Station Five ready to face what I was hoping would be an easy few hours.

As I'm walking into the apparatus bay, Rob is there with a very serious look on his face. I knew I was on time, so I asked him what was going on.

"I'm really sorry about this, but Mike [the captain] has an appointment downtown so you will be acting captain until he gets back."

I'm a new firefighter, and I'm starting to question my strategy of becoming a relief driver, since I'm now realizing that one of the duties of the engineer is to take over the captain's duties when needed. We all knew that possibility existed, but what were the odds that as a relief driver, you would actually be put in that position?

The sweat had to be visible on my forehead when Captain Mike came out to the engine room. He was very apologetic and full of encouragement for this rookie who found himself way over his head before he even got my bunker gear on the unit. About that time, Larry Doan, the battalion chief pulls up behind the station on his daily firehouse mail run. Now, I'm feeling like a hooker in church. Just as we're all saying hi to the chief, the alarm tones go off, and all I'm thinking is "Don't let me screw up, please, don't let me screw up!"

Dispatcher Mark, (a.k.a. Wheels) comes over the engine room speaker . . . "Engine Five, Engine One, Engine Three,

Truck One, Battalion Chief One, structure fire at the apartment complex 2200 Vineyard Avenue, multiple calls received."

I've the Pulse and Chim Chim with me as firefighters. They both come running out of the station faster than I ever saw either one of them move. Things are happening at light speed now; Mike and Rob shrug their shoulders in a "You got this!" gesture, and the chief runs out to his Suburban to head to the call.

Just as I finish getting dressed and go "responding," Wheels is giving me updates: "Engine Five, PD is on scene with flames coming from the roof of the second story," and I reply "Copy, upgrade all units to code 3." The Pulse is now bumped up to acting engineer, and seems to be taking forever getting dressed, so I kindly ask him if he could pick up the pace a little since I didn't have rank or seniority to tell a senior guy what I wanted to say.

Finally, he gets up in the driver's seat and after pushing the starter button a few times, he looks at me with a look of panic and bewilderment and says, "It isn't starting!"

He says he knows what to do, they have been having this problem with the starter sticking: he just needs to bang on it with a wrench. All this time I'm getting updates from Wheels .. . "PD is now reporting victims trapped" and "Police helicopter is reporting exposures to the south are now fully involved."

This is rapidly becoming the biggest fire I will have ever seen, if he can just get the pumper started! He keeps banging on the starter, and it becomes apparent we're not going to be first on scene in our own area. Besides the frantic activities in my head trying to not look like a complete idiot, I couldn't help but think of all the shit I would be taking for years to come.

After what seemed an eternity, he pops up and says he has one more trick to try, and runs away! I can't believe this is happening to me, and I'm thinking that I will never trade with Rob G Rob ever again. I get on the radio, "Dispatch, we're having mechanical difficulties, advise second in unit they will be first on scene" I'm hanging my head low, wondering how bad and in how many ways did I screw this up, and what price was I going to pay?

That was when Mike, the Pulse, Rob G Rob, and Chief Doan came walking up to the captain's window of the pumper, laughing their asses off. They had switched all the radios to a training channel, and set it up with Wheels to dispatch this mother of all calls, so that nobody else would hear the radio traffic and think a real fire was going down!

After a good deal of laughing and finger pointing, my heart started beating again, and I was left wondering how many years of my life I had just lost. Rob went to his appointment, and Captain Mike never had a meeting downtown so we all went into the kitchen for a cup of coffee and a "table critique" of the biggest fire that never happened!

Wayne on the left with Rob G Rob many years ago

SURVIVOR

My pal Scooby was on the job a long time. His dad, "Papa", was also a long-time engineer with our department. I knew Scooby before he was hired from various department off duty events and always got a kick out of working with him after he joined our department. He was a great firefighter and paramedic and whenever our paths would cross on a shift together, we would have a fun time.

Scooby got his name—and remember, no one ever gets a nickname on the FD that they didn't deserve—for the way he talks when he gets excited.

Yup, he sounds exactly like Scooby-Doo!

He was assigned to Station Five, the busiest in the city. It's a four-person firehouse, with a captain, engineer, and two firefighters. It sits right next to a busy interstate highway and has a tremendous amount of old apartment buildings in its first-in area and is close to another city we run automatic aid with. Engine Five runs a *lot* of calls.

Scooby was addicted to the TV show *Survivor*. Since Engine Five was so busy, they would record every episode just in case. He even sent away for an official *Survivor* headband that he would wear for every show! Well, the firehouse being the firehouse, the crew found a way to screw with Scooby's obsession.

They found an extra remote for the TV. They taped down the cable button and then duct taped it to the bottom of the recliner's flip up foot rest. It worked like a charm! Every time the handle was pulled and the foot rest would come up, the TV would go fuzzy as it clicked off the cable!

Of course, his crew couldn't wait for 8 p.m. They made a hug pot of popcorn and told Scooby they couldn't wait to see who was going to be the winner. It was the final episode! They all bet him who would win.

They turned on the TV and all settled in to the recliners with popcorn and drinks. The captain came up with an excuse to call Scooby in to his office right as the show started. Scooby was frantic! After a few minutes the captain relented and they both went in to the TV room to watch with the other two firefighters.

Scooby dished up some popcorn and settled in to the chair. When he flipped up his foot rest the TV went to fuzz.

"*Noo!*" he yelled.

One of the guys got up and messed with the TV and asked Scooby for his help.

They got the TV back on, Scooby went back to his La-Z-Boy chair, flipped up the foot rest and . . .

"No! What the hell is going on?"

Scooby was now flipping out! And the boys could barely hold their smiles in. Someone suggested that maybe the rookie on the other shift hadn't paid the cable bill. That's a firehouse staple: blaming the other shift's rookie for everything.

This went on for the entire episode. He never caught on that each time he flipped up his chair, the TV went off. Scooby lost it and called his wife to make sure she was recording it at home.

They finally let him in on the prank and let him watch the final ten minutes to see who won. But they never let him in on how they kept predicting who would be voted off of the island each episode. The crew would all bet cans of soda on who would get booted off of the island. Scooby always ended up buying for the other three firefighters each episode. He never, ever caught on that they were calling a relative in New York, that got the show three hours ahead each week.

They knew the outcome every single episode. Scooby bought a *lot* of Cokes that season!

THE EL CAP CAPER

Part One: Let's Go Flying

My longtime friend Mark is a world-champion skydiver. We have been on a lot of adventures together over the years. One day he called me at the firehouse and wanted to know if I wanted to make a BASE jump off of El Capitan in Yosemite. I couldn't really turn that down, as I had never been to the park and had been wanting to make my first fixed object jump for a while. He was going to fly over from Arizona and spend a week with me. What could possibly go wrong!

I picked Mark up at the airport and we headed down to Long Beach. We stopped at a sporting goods store to get a few camping supplies we would need for our trip. He excitedly told me the plan. We would drive up to Yosemite, park at night and set up camp. The next day we would hike up from the campground and get to the top of El Cap and jump at dusk. I started to get a little worried, but heard his plan out and it seemed legit.

Part Two: The Jump!

The next day we relived our harrowing experience over coffee. But we had work to do. Mark had a BASE rig, a one-parachute system with a special made canopy just for BASE jumping. I was going to jump my skydiving rig, which has two parachutes, but the main one isn't proper for a BASE jump, as it tends to be erratic on opening. Not a big deal in the sky, but a really big deal when you're jumping off of a 3,200-foot cliff made of granite!

Mark had brought an older, soft opening canopy to put in my rig. We took off the deployment bag a parachute usually goes into on a regular skydive rig and just free stowed the lines. I asked Mark if he had ever jumped a set up like this this.

Nope.

What could possibly go wrong! Looks good on paper. Me first I guess!

We packed up the rig, loaded our gear into my old Toyota pickup truck, known as the Rolling Hilton as I lived in it for a while in Arizona and on a lot of road trips, and headed north.

I had never been to Yosemite before. Now I'm sure you have all seen photos, especially the Ansel Adams ones. But damn! We got into the park at dark, and there it was. All 3,200 feet of awesomeness. I was secretly getting scared as hell.

We set up camp and went to the village for a few beers. I couldn't believe how amazing both El Cap and Half dome were.

The next morning was the moment of truth! We woke up to an incredible day. We went to the village to get a few small food items and water for the hike. Mark was insistent that whatever trash we had, we were jumping it with us back down, so we got all sorts of food in small cellophane bags.

My stomach was churning. We ate some lunch and started our hike. We made it up in a few hours. What a great hike. What a sight. We had a few hours of sunlight until dusk, so we walked the entire edge of El Cap along the nose of it. The view as absolutely incredible!

As the sun started to go down, we looked out for any park rangers and got our rigs out of the backpacks. The plan was to jump and land across the meadow, by the river, stash our gear, and hike out. We would come back later in the night and get it after we hiked back to get the Rolling Hilton.

I was scared shitless now!

Mark had been giving me tips on how to exit the rock, get into a track, and get away from the wall for opening.

"Hey, Mark?"

"Yeah."

"Just how many BASE jumps have you done so far?" I'm expecting him to say like fifteen or twenty.

"Um . . . like about four or five."

WHAT!

we were probably the culprits. We had a good laugh and they offered to take us climbing and then take us up the nose of El Cap. We really wanted to but didn't have the time. Mark knew they were pretty famous climbers. I wish I could remember who they were.

The next morning, I learned about the true force of a bear. As we got to the parking lot, there was a four door Saturn with the back door ripped off. It looked like the fire department had gone to work on it with the jaws of life. The owner was a college student form Connecticut. She had driven across the country visiting all the national parks. She had left a jar of peanut butter in her back seat. Bears are so smart, and Yogi recognized the peanut butter as yummy! The doors were ripped off and the windows smashed. A park ranger came over. He was pretty upset with her and wrote a citation, as she stood there crying, wondering to anyone that would listen how this could have happened to her.

It was time for us to exit stage left! We went back to look for his gear. We searched for a few hours to no avail. On his first cliff jump he loses a borrowed BASE rig. Classic Mark!

We drove out of the park and back to Long Beach. I was so worn out from the adrenaline and was glad we lived and didn't get nabbed!

What a couple of dumbasses!

Jumping a cliff in Italy with Mark a few years later

ANGEL FALLS

I was skydiving every chance I had in the early '90s and was racking up the jumps quickly. In 1996 I had a chance to build a bar and restaurant at a large skydiving center in Arizona. Owning a joint like that was always one of my dreams in life. I teamed up with two partners, Sissy, who had run a small snack bar there on-site, and Littleman, a good skydiving friend from Canada.

I spent weeks designing the restaurant, as we were going to build it from scratch. My longtime friend from high school, Rick, owned a large steel company in Pennsylvania. I sent the plans to him and he said he could ship it out, in pieces, and we could assemble it like an erector set. I sent him the plans and a month later, it was all on a flatbed trailer on its way.

It took about three months of working on it every day once it arrived. My dad flew out from Ohio to help with the electrical wiring. I had no clue what I was doing building and running a restaurant, but somehow it all worked out. We hired a staff of twenty-six full- and part-time employees and planned on serving breakfast, lunch, dinner, and bar snacks like wings and pizza late into the evenings.

We opened to a rousing success! I took a year off from the fire department to run the business. I was skydiving every single day and running the bar in the evenings, all while living in a small travel trailer at the drop zone.

I hired Steve, who was a skydiver from London, to be the head chef. We became close friends and eventually started BASE jumping together. BASE stands for building, antenna, span, and earth. We went on a couple of epic trips, including jumping some big cliffs in various national parks and a lot of bridges.

I sold the restaurant after about a year and went back to the fire department. Steve traveled around the USA for a while and eventually settled back in the UK. We kept in touch and were planning some fun adventures, but never ever did I think this one would happen . . .

The firehouse phone rings one day; I answer it, and lo and behold, it's Steve on the other end.

"Reaper, do you want to go down and jump Angel Falls in Venezuela with us in November?"

Well hell, I'm not going to turn *that* offer down!

"Yes!"

Steve's good friend, Duane, had been traveling in Brazil and met the owner of a fleet of helicopters. He said he would take us to Angel Falls for two jumps each if we had four jumpers minimum. I told Steve I was in, and he laid out the details.

a year earlier. Adrian was going to be the getaway driver. They carefully planned it all out and added in driving time to each location, plus the time to repack their parachutes. It was a very coordinated operation.

Steve and Duane jumped a 5,000-foot-high antenna and then quickly repacked their canopies, had a cold one, and headed to a tall suspension bridge for jump number two of the evening. They had a successful jump, but Duane landed in some thick mud and needed some help from Steve. Adrian wasn't supposed to do anything in the getaway car but just wait until they came to his parking area. Adrian did a U-turn in front of the cops and got their attention. He picked up a muddy Duane and Steve, but got pulled over. Old Bill—as the police are known by in England—had them get out and open the trunk. He arrested them all for trespassing and some other trumped up charges. They spent the night in the pokey. They were released the next morning; however, the police kept their two BASE rigs.

They all had a pending court date. They sought legal assistance, but the lawyer said this case was a bit over his head and referred them to a really good London attorney. She took the case pro bono because it was so unusual.

At the court hearing, the arresting officer didn't show up. The judge was pretty upset and set another date. The boys were getting a bit antsy, not having their base-jumping gear for over three months now, and wondering if they would ever get it released to them.

On their second appearance, the police officer showed up. He had a witness statement from the bridge tollbooth operator, stating he had been traumatized by watching the boys jump from the bridge. He had some hidden camera footage that showed a couple of people in dark clothing, but you couldn't really make anything out, and it turned out that he had interviewed the tollbooth operator two months after the arrest. It also was revealed that he charged them with some bogus, nonexistent laws. The judge threw the case out and admonished them all, letting Steve, Duane, and Adrian know to never ever appear in his court again!

Their lawyer said they were entitled to compensation of a couple thousand dollars now, or they could take it to the higher court and try to get four times as much. They settled on the money at hand! It paid for their Angel Falls trip!

When they arrived, they had on T-shirts that said: Sponsored by the Avon & Somerset Constabulary.

The boys with their custom T-shirts thanking Old Bill

As we approached Kavak, there it was: a fantastic looking Bell 206 Jet Ranger helicopter was parked by the dirt runway!

We descended for a smooth landing on the gravel and taxied right over and parked by the helicopter. We were met by Rafael, the helicopter pilot, and the Pemon ladies that ran the camp. I was starting to feel better about all this!

We unloaded our gear and the pilot flew off to the little village runway a few miles away to drop off the DVDs and pick up some passengers to go back to the city.

The ladies showed us around and had us pick out our beds. Well, not beds but hammocks with mosquito nets draped over them under a thatched roof open area. After that we met in the little dining hut with Rafael and Raul, the owner of the helicopter. We went over our plans for the week and they said a few more people were meeting us to jump. We paid them our thousand dollars each and discussed the dos and don'ts of the jump.

The excitement was building.

We wandered around a bit and looked up at the mountains. This was one of the most amazing places I had ever seen. The tops of the Tepui mountains are flat with many having small waterfalls cascading down the rocky sides. The camp was surrounded by acres and acres of flat grassland. It was an incredible sight to behold.

But the heat . . . and the bugs! The bugs there could eat through titanium.

The next day we woke up after a restless night's sleep and had some scrambled eggs and coffee. We waited for the plane to come back with two more jumpers. We were anxious to see who it was and if we knew them.

When the aircraft finally arrived in the late morning, out walks one of the biggest characters ever! The one and only Edgar from Ecuador! He had a young jumper with him named Fausto. Both great guys. But Edgar . . . he's a classic!

We met them and planned out our next day. They'll jump first, as it's a bit of a ride out to the falls, and they could only stay one day. They were both jumping skydiving rigs and the gear was ratted out old-student stuff!

Hmmm . . . good luck boys! What could possibly go wrong!

We were then going to go out and jump our first jumps and continue the next day. Everything was ready to go. I knew I wasn't going to sleep a wink that night.

I'm not going to lie—we were all pretty fucking scared.

In the late afternoon a different Cessna flew in with four guys on board. Well, here it is, I thought to myself. This is where we get killed and they take the rest of our cash!

Out jumps a guy named Freddy, Alberto, and two guys whose names I can't remember. They had just been leading a group of Americans through the jungle for twenty-one days. They were sunburned and bitten to hell by bugs. They were friends with Rafael and our helicopter pilot, and all had done some jumps in DeLand, Florida. They just wanted to come out and watch.

Rafael hovered at the top right next to where the water flows over into the abyss, with one skid resting on a big boulder as he gave us the OK to get out and step off of the skids and on to the top of the falls. Steve and I slowly stepped off of the skids and waved him away. He hovered out and spun the helicopter to face us. Alberto was in the front filming us.

My heart was beating out of my chest.

As I stood there with Steve, we marveled at the view. I wondered just how many human beings had ever stood on top of these falls.

One last selfie at the top with Steve before we send it!

The scenery was breathtaking! But enough of that . . . we had to jump.

Steve told me to go first. I had brought a small throw-way drugstore camera. This was in the pre-GoPro, mini camera days. This was all just going to be in our memories.

I gave Steve a high five and wished him a great jump. I thanked him for the adventure and told him I would see him in the landing area. Then I just turned and ran off the ledge. As you can see from the photo, Steve snapped the camera at the exact perfect moment!

Steve captured my exit perfectly. This might be the best photo ever taken by a throw away cardboard camera.

As my body went free of the rock, the "cartoon moment" was incredible! For that millisecond, I marveled at the view. Gravity started sucking me toward the jungle floor—I'm not sure if my heart started racing or if it just stopped. It was spectacular!

I picked up speed and was flying next to the falls, tracking my body away from the mountain. It was an incredible experience. I took a deep delay down into the bowels of the falls before I deployed my parachute.

Exhilarating is the only way I can describe it.

Whack!

My parachute opened rather briskly and I was flying next to the falls, getting droplets of water all over me. It felt great

COTTON BALLS

"But hey, there was some left, I couldn't wash it!"

It doesn't matter what is in the big glass casserole pan
Lasagna, enchiladas, or brownies. There will be a one inch
by two-inch slice left in the corner so no one washes the pan

—Reaper

One day at Station One, it was revealed that the Party Bob hated cotton balls. He was actually afraid of their texture or something. Ever since then, I've discovered that many more people I know have an aversion to cotton balls. You have *got* to be kidding me! But, hey, I can't stand mustard and guys would slab that on my stuff and it would terrify me. Well, actually, the smell almost makes me throw up. They called French's mustard "Reaper kryptonite." I guess we all have our own cross to bear!

The Party Bob came in one day and was looking a little worn down. At lunch time he snuggled into one of the day room recliners for a nice nap. Pike Pole had located a couple bags of cotton balls stashed in behind all of the medic gear in the supply closet. It was game on!

We spread them out all over a snoring Bob and gathered to watch him wake up.

"Hey, Bob, the chief is coming in, wake up!"

He sat up in the recliner and looked at all of the soft, puffy white cotton balls that were all over him. What happened next makes me wish we had cell phones or GoPros back then.

He jumped up, dancing all around, and started swatting at them like they were scorpions and deadly spiders!

Chief Doan, always a prankster himself, came by to watch. Everyone on our entire crew was in tears!

We picked up all of the cotton and saved it for the next shift, when we put them all over his uniform shirts in his locker. He had to get a coat hanger to hook them and soak them in a big pan of water to "kill" them.

Unreal!

I don't get it, but hey, I still hate mustard!

Dennis showed up with the medical gear. I put him on high-flow oxygen. Dennis just kept saying "We're all going to get fired!" Warren told him to just shut the hell up!

So, a little recap. Here we're, on scene for just over twenty minutes. We have a dead guy that came back to life, while waiting for the coroner. About thirty neighbors are on the street out front. We had already cancelled an ambulance and medic fire unit. The sun beating on me was like being in an Amana Radarange. Yup. Twenty-nine years old, ten years on the job, and it's all gonna end right here. Oh yeah, his son and daughter were on the way too.

We worked with a private ambulance company for transport. They had a paramedic we called Rod Stewart because he had the same spiked, mullet-type hairdo. He was the first to show up.

In a smart-assed tone, he asked, "Who called this guy"? I thought the captain was going to punch his lights out!

"I did," he shouted, "now work on him!"

The medic engine showed up and we got the patient into the ambulance and on the way to the hospital. Dennis just wandered around muttering we were all getting fired.

When we pulled back into the station, I grabbed a big glass of water and plopped down in the air-conditioned TV room recliner. Warren told us that there will probably be an investigation and to just tell the truth. He said he would take all the heat for us and that it was his call. If anyone could take the heat it was him, always a stand-up guy. I've worked with a couple of captains that would have been passing the blame to us somehow. But not Warren.

As it turned out, the blanket I used to cover the patient with had the initials "BEE" on it. It had been issued to Bruce, the inspector I worked with in fire prevention. He was a pastor that had left the department after only five years for church life and to run his own flock. Thus, the department nickname for it became the Magic Blanket.

Chuck showed up after his appointment and asked me if anything went on. I told him that no way in hell was I ever coming back to cover for him and to go inside! When we told him the story, he couldn't believe it. I grabbed my gear and headed back down to my firehouse.

When I pulled in, both crews, Engine One and Truck One were waiting out back of the firehouse to hear the story. You see, on the fire department, you can't fart sideways without it getting around. And the guys had heard the dispatch calls. I told them I couldn't talk about it and threw my gear onto the ladder truck and went in to take a shower. I was drenched in sweat. And then over the PA system, "Firefighter Grimm to the BC's office." Damn that Chuck!

When I went in to see the battalion chief, he wanted to know what had happened. I explained to him that this guy was deader than dead. The chief was calm and it didn't seem like anyone was going to need the union rep. He asked me to write out a statement. When I left his office, I phoned the union president. He had already gotten the news and was on it.

The eighty-two-year-old patient died a day later. There was a postmortem exam done and his brain had been so damaged in the fall that he would have never been able to function normally again. He was dead no matter what we would have done.

We all learned a lesson that day and department policy was changed for confirming death. The paramedic unit would now always have to come in and declare the death. We knew a few other times in the past that a similar situation had happened, so it was the right decision by the EMS chief.

For many years after this call, we would be on scene and somebody would be shot dead or dead from a motorcycle accident or terrible auto accident and some smart ass would say:

"Hey Reaper, this person needs the Magic Blanket!"

FLU SHOTS

O ver the years, Jethro Bodine became one of my closest friends on the job. I could probably write my next book filled with just his stories! A few years after he was hired, he bought a house a few blocks down the street from Station One. He would often ride his skateboard to work, listening to his head phones and wearing his beloved Guns N' Roses jean jacket.

Bodine has a great sense of humor, which he inherited from his mom. He grew up in the city and knew absolutely everyone in town. We ended up together on the truck company for years. He drove the front, and I was the tillerman. The only thing I really miss about the job is steering that behemoth through traffic with him, air horn and siren blaring, heading to an emergency. I used to tell him we could sell a ride on the truck for $10,000 on eBay! He could wedge the rig through traffic like no other engineer on the job.

Bodine is one of those guys that sees the funny in most everything. He has pulled some classic pranks, so this won't be the last story he will be in for sure.

A buddy of mine came to visit the station one day when we were making spaghetti. He watched Bodine tuck a towel under his chin and mow down about three plates of it. He nicknamed him Jethro Bodine after *The Beverly Hillbillies* character that could eat like a horse. The name has stuck forever.

One day we were both called in to work an overtime shift at Station One. We didn't have much food in the station and he called his mom to bring him some food. His mom was the sweetest, funniest lady you could ever meet. After a few minutes with her, you saw where he got his sense of humor. She showed up with a 21-piece bucket of Kentucky Fried Chicken, a giant bag of potato chips, and a two-liter bottle of Coke. I walked in the kitchen when he was starting to devour it.

"Hey, your mom brought us some food, what do I owe you?"

He looked at me like I was crazy. "What the hell, Bodine, you're not going to eat all of this by yourself are you"?

"OK, Reaper, I'll give you some." I got a wing, a leg, a thigh, a glass of Coke, and some chips! He mauled the rest.

We can't remember what flu it was a few years ago that had everyone so damned scared and getting shots. Swine flu, bird flu, we both can't remember. The department employed a nurse that helped oversee the paramedic program. She had set up a table in the basement of the firehouse to give out flu shots to the city employees for free. It was lunchtime, and at every firehouse in America, lunchtime means a quick eat and then a long nap. The city hall is right next door to the firehouse.

People kept coming in looking for the shots and waking the crews up. Well, Bodine had enough and sprang into action.

He set up a table in front of the apparatus room doors in front of the station. He put a sign on it that said "Flu shots here." He grabbed the biggest needles he could find out of the medic supply room and grabbed a surgical mask and some latex gloves. He got the gloves dirty with some old motor oil. He had his props all laid out. Alcohol swabs, Band-Aids, needles, etc. He set a lone chair at the end of the table next to the giant needles.

The first "victim" came over from city hall. Bodine asked her to have a seat. He acted like he didn't have a clue what he was doing. He told the lady not to worry, he had taken an eight-hour class on giving shots, but this was his first time on a real patient. He wrapped the rubber band on her arm and swabbed it. He made his hand shake as he approached with the needle and then he dropped it on the ground! He picked it up and brushed it off and told her not to worry.

She said, "Oh, hell no," and jumped up and hurried back to city hall!

The next victim came over. She had a sweater on. Bodine asked her why she had a sweater on, as it was "shot day." He told her not to worry, as he could just give the shot through her sweater because the needle was so sharp! She hurried off back to city hall too.

A few more city employees came over. On one of them, he had bent the needle, dropped it on the ground and picked it back up, and brushed it off and bent it back sort of straight.

The lady told him no way in hell was he touching her with that needle and death by the flu would be better! A few of the city hall staff had finally figured out this was just a gag and cracked up.

Word got out at city hall, and the nurse giving the real shots found out. Then, the city manager called over to the fire chief to see what the hell was happening Well, of course, here it comes: "Engineer Mayfield to the chief's office"

When he went in the chief's office, he got a pretty good grilling. However, the chief knew all about it and actually thought it was pretty funny. So, after a stern threat of days off, which Bodine thought was good because he was out of sick and vacation time as usual, the chief told him to knock it off.

The chief thought it was one of the best pranks in a long time.

The city manager wasn't quite as amused.

THE BIG HOUSE CHRONICLES

We should run the fire department like the airlines. You
want a paramedic, that's a $50 first-aid surcharge. You
want water in the tank, that's a $30 hydrant charge. Oh,
you're on the fourth floor and need a ladder truck, that's a
$100 elevation tax. And don't forget your $25 "911" user fee.
Thank you for frying with us today!

—Reaper

Station One was the department headquarters. It housed
the fire prevention bureau, the chief and assistant chief's
offices, the training and paramedic captains and chiefs, the
secretaries, and Engine One, Truck One, and Battalion One.

The station was built in the 1950s and didn't have many
windows. There were two basements, one on each side of the
firehouse that didn't have a connecting hallway. They must
have built it out of the thick cement block to survive an attack
by the Russians during the cold war. The police department's
headquarters was next door, and city hall was half a block

away. The emergency dispatch offices were in the basement of the police offices. There was always a lot of activity going on around the firehouse.

At the time I worked there, we had six total fire stations and only two of the units had paramedic firefighters. Engine One and Engine Three at our training center, thus making those two pumpers incredibly busy. We were the only ladder truck in the city, so our unit responded to every fire call and rescue, including auto extrications. The other units would have to stop in after fires to fill their breathing apparatus tanks, as we housed the only compressor. The bomb-squad unit was parked there along with a utility pickup truck. As you can imagine, it was a beehive of activity and a lot of fun. The twenty-four-hour shifts usually passed pretty quickly at the Big House.

It was one block north of the main east-west avenue and a couple of blocks east of the main north-south boulevard in town. We had access quickly to the rest of town. Because Engine One had two paramedic firefighters on board, and we were the only truck company, the entire city was our "first due" area. Some shifts we were running thirty to forty calls out of Station One, and it seemed we had no shortage of fires, gang violence, or medical-aid calls. It was a great place to gain a lot of on-the-job practical experience.

One: "That looks like your truck!"

Car thefts were a thing in the neighborhood back then, and even though we were right next door to the cop shop, the thieves would still try to steal cars in the back parking lot or break into the staff cars. There was a vacant lot across the street that the city fenced in for all of us to park in. It had a gate we would lock every evening and that seemed to keep trouble away. I bought a pickup truck to drive to work, as the car thieves tried to steal my Corvette from behind the station but must have been interrupted by a police car coming in. The city finally put cameras up in the parking lot for some extra security.

One shift we were all playing basketball behind the firehouse in the late afternoon. The Viking had just bought a brand-new diesel, crew cab pickup truck to tow his boat. In the middle of the game, we looked through the engine room and there was a truck that looked exactly like his speeding away. Sure enough, we glanced over to the parking area and his truck was gone! Some ballsy thief stole it while we were right across the street playing hoops!

The Viking jumped in the utility truck to chase him and we called dispatch right away. My only thought was, Who gets the bad guy first, the police, or the Viking!

He was the strongest guy on our department by far, and when he got mad, there was no way I would want to be the recipient of his rage. The police finally nabbed the bad guy miles away in the next city to the west. Luckily for him, it was the cops and not the Viking that got to him first!

Two: "Was that gunfire?"

I was sitting in the TV room watching a hockey game one afternoon. The rest of the crew was in the basement working out and playing ping-pong. I was half asleep when I heard a "pop, pop." I didn't think anything of it, it sounded like a car backfiring, and there was an auto repair shop across the street always wrenching and making noise. Then I realized it was a Sunday and they weren't open.

I opened the big firehouse apparatus doors and there was a man lying on the sidewalk with two bullets lodged in his rear end! I paged the crew to come help patch this poor man up and notified the dispatch center about the drive by. He was standing right in front of the only window in our TV room when he was hit. He probably kept a small caliber bullet from flying in the only window and towards the recliner I was in. Nothing like a drive-by in front of the firehouse next door to the police station.

Maybe now I see why we didn't have too many windows at Station One!

Three: "Out of town crooks!"

There is a hamburger fast-food restaurant called Andy's Burgers a block away from the firehouse. It's the typical walk-up, drive-through joint like hundreds of others across Southern California. Gyros, burgers, chili dogs, tacos, and fries are the staple items. We would stop in now and then on a busy shift when we had no time to prepare dinner.

I was working one Saturday afternoon and standing in front of the station talking with Horrible, my new truck company firefighter partner. We were good friends and laughing about something when we heard the tires squeal a block away. Some moron had just pulled a gun and robbed Andy's. This guy was an out-of-towner for sure, because, seriously, who robs a hamburger place one block from the main police station!

A patrol car was just coming back at shift change when he saw what was happening at the walk-up window. The armed robber saw him and bolted to his running car that was in the alley for a getaway, no cash in hand. The officer radioed dispatch, and since it was shift change, there were about forty-five police officers in the parking lot behind the firehouse. The oncoming and offgoing officers were all there!

The idiot flies up the street and about ten squad cars start after him. We could hear the sirens head up the street and then turn to the east. We couldn't believe it; the fool drove right back towards the firehouse and police station with the entire posse in tow. And then, he did one of the dumbest moves ever to get away from the police. There was a one-way driveway that you could go out onto the street from the police-car parking area, but it had the big metal spikes that kept cars from coming in that way. Horrible and I ran to the back of the firehouse to keep watching this almost cartoon like ordeal.

Yup!

The idiot hit the brakes into a skid and turned left into the one-way driveway behind the police station! All four of his tires blew instantly as he hit the spikes and he came to a wheel smoking stop, met with about fifteen officers with guns drawn, ten feet away from the entrance to the jail. This was *way* before cell phones with cameras and it's a shame, because we could have made this fiasco go viral.

What a dumbass!

Four: "Sorry!"

Before we had direct deposit for our pay, the checks were given out every two weeks at the reception desk at Station One. Working a payday Friday was always fun, because we would see coworkers from other stations and shifts and get filled in on the latest happenings from around the six firehouses.

It was a payday Friday when Norm, one of the captains from Engine Four, was on his way to pick up his check when the police pulled him over a couple of blocks away. They had guns drawn and made him get out of his truck and get down on the street, face down. A couple of other patrol cars came screaming in to assist. Norm yelled to them that he was a captain on the fire department so please don't shoot! Finally, a few of the officers recognized him. The rash of local bank robberies were still happening, and his red truck fit the description of the getaway vehicle of a bank that had just been robbed.

"We're really sorry, Norm!" The officers were pretty apologetic.

I spent six years assigned to Truck One. I had a hell of a lot of fun at that station and lots of stories came out of my time there. All good things must come to an end, and I eventually transferred down to Engine Three with Joey, Hop, and the Bhagwan.

THE CUP

Our LA Blazers hockey team was becoming a bit more competitive in the Canadian firefighter tournaments. We had come a long way since that first year when we got killed every game. We were an anomaly that first tournament: hockey players from California. We were like the Jamaican bobsled team!

Our friendship with the Prince George team that we met during our first tournament was growing. Each year we would stay at the same hotel and have a lot of fun hanging out together. We all started to become really good friends.

Over the years we have gone up there to play charity games against them and have been involved in a *lot* of fun and mayhem together over the decades of friendship.

One year the Prince George team won their division in the tournament. They were at the bar with all of us and celebrating their big win.

While I distracted them with a round of Kamikaze shots, my partner in crime, Gerry O', stole their trophy and slipped it out to our rental car. It was a perfect heist. Not one of their guys noticed that they left the bar empty handed.

The plan was to take photos of the trophy living it up, on a beach towel in Redondo Beach, at an LA Kings game, etc. As we boarded the plane with their trophy at the Vancouver airport, we ran into none other than Emilio Esteves, who had just ended filming *Mighty Ducks 2*.

Boarding the plane with Gerry O', Scott, and Emilio Esteves
with the Cup

So, the first photo we took with the cup was with Coach Bombay!

We were all wondering what would happen when we handed them the trophy back a year later. They had some pretty big tough guys, and of course, they would know it was Gerry O' or me that stole their trophy.

Luckily, they all took it in great stride and laughed their asses off over it all.

Whew!

We won the tournament two years later in Calgary. We assigned two of our biggest rookies on the team to guard the cup with their lives! It made the rounds to the local bars under very strict protection.

The Prince George players tried to nab it, but we prevailed and took it home with us!

The friendships we have had with those guys have been incredible over all these years. We get together once in a while to put a team in the old fart Over 50 Division. We know most of the players from Vancouver, Kamloops, and Calgary, as they have all been in the tournament for thirty or forty years.

It has now turned into a lot of beer, stories, and pizza, mixed in with a little hockey. And we're OK with that!

THE BET

When we hosted a couple firefighter tournaments in Las Vegas, we had teams participate from the FDNY, Calgary, Kamloops, Vancouver, Prince George, and Chicago. The team from Chicago was called the Chicagoland Hosers, made up of players from the Windy City suburbs and a couple Chicago city firefighters. Like the Prince George players, these guys were a real collection of personalities!

We met them in the bar after the game and hit it off right away. After years of playing in tournaments, our team and the Chicagoland team have created a special friendship that's kind of magical. The Chicago boys told us about a tournament in the Toronto area every year and invited us to come there to play in it. The tourney was every February, so it didn't conflict with our other tournament in Western Canada.

We went every year to Toronto, and if we couldn't get a full team to go, we would join the Hosers. It was always a great time in Toronto with those guys, and I could probably write an entire book on these tournaments, but I'm not sure the statutes of limitations are up yet! Skating with the Chicago team was always a great time, and we often did well in the tournaments.

One year we took a really strong LA Blazers team. It worked out that all of the better players could make it, and so we plowed our way through the preliminary games, going undefeated, and met a strong Toronto-area team in the final game.

The Chicago team was in our division, but were knocked out early from a playoff spot. Their entire team came to the rink for the final game to cheer us on to a big victory.

Our teams from Los Angeles were always a bit of an anomaly, having guys that could actually play hockey from SoCal, and would often draw a crowd of curious onlookers. This game had a large group of people watching to see how we would hold up against a strong Canadian team.

We played a really hard-fought game and lost by a goal. As we went through the handshake line, some of the Chicago players came out on the ice to congratulate us on a game well played.

That's when we got the news . . .

Johnny R, a Chicago firefighter, and good pal of ours, had made a big bet with a teammate that we would lose the championship game. When we found out, we approached him.

"Hey, Johnny, I hear you bet against us this morning!"

Johnny R was on the ice, in his street clothes, and the look on his face told it all. He knew he was doomed! He started to run off of the ice, slipping in his shoes, to no avail!

We grabbed him and shred his shirt and pants off! This was on the rink that had about 200+ other players that were watching from the upstairs bar! They all rushed to the window on our rink side to watch.

We dragged Johnny R, now just in just his tighty-whities, around the rink by his ankles. He was laughing his ass off and begging for forgiveness and mercy! The crowd upstairs in the bar was roaring in approval. Then we dragged him into the net, and started shooting pucks, rather softly, at him.

Johnny R was still laughing and pleading for forgiveness!

We dragged him to the bench, with the ice shavings sliding down his underwear, and told him the only way he was getting off so easily was if he used his $100 winnings to buy us all beer.

He easily agreed.

THE INTERPRETER

I was working my fourth or fifth twenty-four-hour shift in a row. It was summertime, so a lot of firefighters were on vacation and we had a couple of guys out on injury. I couldn't get a day off, along with a lot of other firefighters.

I was sent to work on Engine Five in the morning. Of course, that was my assignment the day of the Magic Blanket incident, so on the way up I was wondering what mayhem would happen there today.

When I got to the firehouse the captain, engineer, and other firefighter were all also filling in. We had an entire crew of firefighters who had been on duty for days. All great guys though, so it was going to be fun, even if everyone of us was a little worn down.

Station Five is pretty busy; it started off at shift change, call after call. We ran on a few medical aids and a minor traffic accident. And then we got a call for an injured subject at an apartment building.

We rolled out of the firehouse and weaved our way through the morning traffic to the complex. We found the apartment number and knocked on the door. A young Korean girl, about eighteen or nineteen, answered the door just wearing a robe. We walked in to find a young Korean man writhing in pain on the floor. He only had a pair of gym shorts on.

"What's the problem, sir"? The captain asked.

"Ma Ba Ha!" he yelled.

"What?"

"Ma BA HA!"

"Sir, I don't understand."

"MY BA HAAA!"

He was rolling on the floor writhing in pain, holding his private parts.

"MA BA HAAA!"

Then it dawned on me.

"Sir, do your balls hurt?"

"Ya, Ya!" he said, shaking his head yes.

We asked him to pull down his shorts and show us.

He pulled his pants down and we all got a look. All four of us just winced and went "Oooooh."

His testicles were the size of oranges!

"Sir, how did this happen?"

The kid just pointed to the bathroom. He was in agony.

I looked in the bathroom and there was the culprit. A sink pulled out of the wall.

The young girl was turning as red as our fire truck!

They had been having wild, morning monkey sex on the bathroom sink when it let go from the wall without warning. She came down on the family jewels, pinching them on the sink. That's gonna leave a mark!

The ambulance company arrived and took the poor kid off to the ER.

We jumped back on the rig and couldn't stop laughing. We were all in sympathy pain with the poor kid though. The captain said we should hit the store while we were out and get our dinner grub. We cooked up some nice steaks that night to celebrate our intact family jewels.

Sex injuries . . .

UNITED AIRLINES

When things go bad, always blame the rookie
on the other shift.

—Everyone

Every firehouse around the world has had issues with the fire equipment running into the big apparatus bay doors. Some bay doors are on timers to close after a few minutes and some departments use remotes for the crew to shut the door after clearing them. Many a firehouse door has been ripped off of the track or been run into over the years across the globe!

We worked with a captain named Jordan. Hell of a nice guy, but he had his quirks. He always thought everyone was out to get him, and he had some unique ways about him, to put it mildly. I never minded working with him as it was always pretty entertaining.

He worked at Station Four. The bay doors were on a timer there; it also was wired into a traffic signal in front of the station. When you would hit the timer, the light would turn red to stop all of the traffic on the street, and then the big bay door would come down after three or four minutes.

His crew had caught the closing door a number of times with the deck gun, the big water cannon looking thing on the top of the pumper that can shoot hundreds of gallons of water per minute. The driver always managed to stop before tearing the doors off completely and breaking the windows.

It happened one more time. They were taking a little longer to get into their gear before heading out to the call. The engineer this time was new to the station and didn't catch that the door was closing so . . . CRASH!

They did some pretty major damage. The door came off of the tracks and broke some pieces off of the rails and wheels. The battalion chief was really pissed off as this had happened too many times on the same shift. The captain was nervous as hell and knew he would probably be getting a written reprimand.

He looked for an excuse, and boy did he come up with a good one!

There's a big airport right in the center of town. It's pretty busy and the airliners take off to the west on most days, flying just a bit south of Station Four. The captain made a few calls and had come up with his "defense."

When the chief stopped by, Jordan proceeded to plead his case. He explained to the chief, who listened with a straight face to the entire spiel, that an airliner had departed at the same time as the fire call. The pilot was talking on the radio and the door remote is probably on the same frequency. He explained to the chief that it wasn't really his fault that the guys took way too long to get out of the station before the timer closed the door. It was all United Airlines fault for talking to the control tower on departure!

The chief just looked at him in awe while such bullshit was being spouted.

"Here's your written reprimand, just sign it!"

"But, Chief . . ."

"Well, Cap, in thirty years on the job, I have to hand it to you, this was a spectacular theory, but I'm not buying any of it!"

A few weeks later they changed the system, putting a remote for the door in the jump seats for the firefighters to operate department wide.

Problem solved.

PAY HIM THE DOLLAH!

My buddy Jackie is one of a kind. He's a retired captain from the LAFD. He was raised in Brooklyn and grew up playing hockey and boxing in the Golden Glove ranks. He skated on our Blazer teams for quite a while and was a pretty good goal scorer. Plus, he took no crap from anyone on the ice. He is now a world-famous boxing referee and has handled a lot of big name fights over the years, including the heavyweight championships.

On one of our hockey trips to Canada we had to stop at the airport in Salt Lake City. We were walking through the terminal and saw this sort of dumpy looking dude walking slowly with a tall, statuesque-looking blonde girl with fantastic legs. I was walking next to Jackie and we both turned to watch her stroll away.

"Holy crap, that was Robin Leach!" Jackie blurted out loudly when they had just gone past us.

"No, it wasn't," I said. "Why would Robin Leach be flying commercial and not in a private jet?"

"It was, it was!" Jackie was being an excited little school girl seeing the host of *Lifestyles of the Rich and Famous*. A comical sight coming from such a New York tough guy!

"Wasn't," I said.

"It was, it was. I'll bet you a dollar it was him!"

"OK, I'll bet you a dollar it's not Robin Leach."

Jackie takes off running after him down the terminal hallway.

"Mr. Leach, Mr. Leach, tell him it's you, tell him it's you!"

I chased after him.

And I'll be damned . . .

Robin Leach himself turned around and looked me right in the eye, pointed to Jackie, and said in his very British accent:

"Pay him the dollah!"

THE SON OF REAPER

It was the summer of 1988. Southern California was having another hot and smoggy July. Down on Holt Blvd, a major east-west street in the city, we were experiencing a ton of medical calls and fires. The street had used car dealerships, old mobile-home parks, stores, small bars and restaurants, and a host of old abandoned hotels, plus lots of apartment buildings and little bungalows.

We were responding out of Station One to all sorts of mayhem. Shootings, stabbings, medical emergencies and a *lot* of fires. It seemed that every Saturday night a group of kids would be burning down a vacant old hotel or house. There was a lot of gang activity going on also.

It was a great place to get some serious experience.

The department only had six stations at that time and only Engine One and Engine Three had paramedic firefighters assigned to them, so they ran with the nonmedic units on all medical calls all across the city. (Today all ten stations have two paramedics on each engine company.)

The Engine One boys were out on a call when we got dispatched over the firehouse loudspeaker.

"Truck One, possible childbirth."

AAARRRGH! We all groaned in unison.

Childbirth of your own children might be a beautiful thing, but not in the back of a bungalow on Holt Blvd in searing summer heat.

Norm fired up the ladder truck and off we went down Holt Blvd. We were responding with the private ambulance company only, since both of our paramedic units were busy. We pulled up in front of the small group of bungalows and the Geez was trying to sort out what little house we were supposed to go to. We figured out, after a little conversation over the radio with our dispatch center, that we were supposed to go to the back house on the left.

We grabbed our first-aid and childbirth-kits, plus the resuscitator oxygen bottle and knocked on the door.

This giant biker-looking dude answered the door.

"She's in the bathroom," he said, in an annoyed tone.

That's all he said to us as he pointed the way.

I went into the bathroom and there was the patient. She was sitting on the toilet and moaning in agony. She had a big T-shirt on, nothing else.

The stench. Oh, the stench!

I asked her how far along in her pregnancy and all the other pertinent childbirth questions. She seemed to be stoned out of her mind. She mumbled incoherent answers to my questions. Her teeth were mostly all gone, probably from years of meth use.

She let out a big scream and said the baby was coming!

Crap!

We're going to have to deliver this kid right here. Without an ambulance and a paramedic unit. And I know just who will have to be at the business end of it all, as the Geez and Norm wanted no part of this! Norm was out on the curb waiting to guide the ambulance and the Geez, as the captain, was doing the paperwork and talking to dispatch. This was all going to be up to me and my partner that day, Roger.

I lifted up her T-shirt, and much to my disappointment, she was crowning!

Roger helped me get her off of the toilet, out of the bathroom and into the living room. Her biker boyfriend was just sitting in a chair, drinking a beer, and watching TV. He wasn't the least bit interested or fussed.

I asked the Geez if there was an ETA on the ambulance. Nope, they're all on other calls.

Damn!

We got the childbirth kit out and prepared for an imminent delivery. By now both Roger and I were sweating in the heat of the house. I noticed something moving in a big glass case on the floor. As I turned to look—*holy crap*! There was a huge python snake in it slithering around.

I just wanted this call to be over. Sweat was dripping off me. The house was a dump and the soon to be mom is tweaking and the dad is drunk. What a Hallmark card moment.

The patient is now screaming and writhing in pain. The head of the baby is popping out and contracting back in. I'm thinking that with all of her past drug use, this kid is probably coming out with some missing body parts.

Just then, the dark clouds parted and there was sunshine!

In walks our regular shift paramedics, Pike Pole and Rob G Rob to the rescue with all of their medic gear!

They heard the angst in the Geez calling dispatch for an ambulance update and cleared the call they were on. The Viking rolled them across town warp speed in the pumper to help us out.

About five minutes later an ambulance arrived. She still hadn't delivered yet and they got her to the hospital quickly. Just as the guys rolled her into the ER, incredibly, she popped out a healthy baby boy.

Every time we would pass that house on Holt, Pike Pole or one of the other guys would ask me, "How's the son of Reaper doing?"

Hahahaha, really funny guys those friends of mine.

About three years later I was working with a different shift, but with Pike Pole as my partner, and we received a call for a medical emergency at the same address. A couple had just moved into the front house and the wife was having labor pains.

"Hey Reaper, you're gonna have twin sons at this place!"

A funny guy that Pike Pole.

Just then, we saw this little blonde kid, about three years old, running around in the driveway. He only had a diaper on and was dirty as hell.

His mom came out to yell at him. Sure enough, it was her, and the baby we almost delivered. It was the son of Reaper! The little bugger ran away from his mom and she had to chase him. It was the same lady. It was confirmed.

The kid was a holy terror!

The husband of the pregnant lady we were loading up into the ambulance was just shaking his head. He said that the little kid had been coming up and pulling his diaper down and pooping on their front porch every day! He told us what terrible neighbors they were and wished they had known about all of the parties and bikers before they moved in. They were looking to move after only a few weeks in their place.

His wife didn't have that baby on the call this day. Damn. I really needed a . . . son of Pike Pole.

1152 Holt Blvd. It's a vacant field now.

Some places and calls you just never forget!

THE ELEVATOR

The summer games were being held at the old Belmont rink in the Bay Area. We had a pretty stacked team, and we were anxious to hand the San Francisco team a punishing defeat in front of their huge hometown crowd, all in the name of raising money for the St. Francis Burn Center. It didn't matter. These games were war.

We had a new rookie player on our team, Jimmy, who was like every little brother in the world. He was a great kid, but would get under our skin every once in a while. Well, nearly every day actually!

The day before the games started, we were all in my room having beer and pizza. Jimmy was just jabbing at everyone with a hockey stick and being ridiculously silly. I told him he had better stop or he was going to ride the elevator.

Well . . .

Being the little shit instigator he was, he started really messing with me and a couple of the other guys on the team, giggling the entire time. That was it. I looked over at my teammates and we started laughing. Yup, it was time to make him ride the elevator.

We tackled him and grabbed our hockey tape rolls out of our gear bags. We found a small chair and stripped him down to his underwear.

We wrapped a couple miles of hockey tape around his arms and feet and taped him to the chair,

We were staying in a hotel that was about twenty-two stories tall. In he went, taped to the chair. We pushed the button for every single floor, including the lobby.

Up to each floor.

Ding. Doors open to laughter.

Ding. More people laughing.

Every ten minutes or so we would go out and push all the buttons again. It seemed some of the hotel patrons were in on it too and they pushed the buttons also!

About a half an hour later here comes a very red faced, almost naked rookie with a hotel security guard looking pretty pissed off.

"I think this guy belongs to you guys," the guard said with his best stern look.

"Yes sir, we don't know how this happened, we'll get him in his room right away, sir!"

The kid never got out of line with the "veteran players" again!

Bomb Squad Tricks

O ur fire department has an EOD unit, the bomb squad. They send team members to the Redstone Arsenal in Alabama for FBI training and do ongoing continuing education at the local and state level. The members are selected to be on the team and are top-notch and get called in to some hairy situations. They also have a supply of detonation cord, C-4, and other goodies.

One day we were all working at Station Three, which is also the training tower station. One of the leaders of the squad had just gotten back from training in Alabama and learned a new trick. The drill tower had a large area around it for spotting equipment and stretching hose to the five-story brick building used for training fires and rescue drills.

"Hey, check this one out you guys!"

Shoe got an old semi tire and filled it with some gasoline. He then wrapped the tire with detonation cord, a cord that explodes all at once when ignited.

Of course, most firefighters are firebugs, so we were eager with anticipation to see what was going to happen.

Shoe put the tire out in the middle of the training tower parking lot. We all stood back and watched with great amusement.

Blam!

The tire just exploded in a ball of fire, and the sidewall of the tire went flinging into the air!

It was like a glorious, flaming Frisbee, twirling up and up. The spinning tire went about a hundred or so feet up in the air. Still flaming. What a sight!

Right up until it started flying, still on fire, toward the big dry grass field next to the station!
It caught the light breeze heading eastward, and off it went away from the drill tower parking lot.

It glided gently over to the large vacant field next door, still spitting spinning flames, and caught the tall, dead scrub brush and tumbleweeds on fire. The dry brush started burning instantly!

We scrambled to the pumper, threw on some safety gear, and rushed next door like a bunch of Three Stooges to put it out!

Luckily, this was way before everyone on the planet had a cell phone, so dispatch didn't receive any calls about it!

We all took a pact: not a word of this to the battalion chief!

Shhhhhh . . .

THANKSGIVING TURKEY AND ALL THE TRIMMINGS

I always enjoyed working on the holidays. When I was at Station One, we had nine firefighters on duty every shift. We would invite our family members down for a giant meal for Christmas or Thanksgiving. Hosting the holiday meals was always a lot of fun, and it was really enjoyable to spend time with everyone's families. One of the great benefits of being on the job is watching everyone's kids grow up. And eventually even working with some of them.

One Thanksgiving Day we were preparing the huge meal right after breakfast. We got the two birds stuffed and in the oven then decided to play some basketball to work up our appetites.

We played hoops, which at our station was more like full-contact basketball, for about two hours and were all a sweaty mess. We went in to the kitchen to get some water and see what we could pick at. The pumpkin pies were calling our names!

Just then, in walks a young man with a giant box.

"Hey, are you guys the firemen that respond to the Hilton Hotel all the time?"

"Yup, we go there on all of the alarms."

"Great, our kitchen manager made all of this for you and wanted me to personally thank you for all the help over the years"

"Gee, thanks kid, tell him thank you very much!"

The Hilton Hotel had a big problem with their fire alarm system, so we went there almost every day on false alarms due to faulty equipment.

We opened the box, and much to our delight, there was a cooked turkey, mashed potatoes, and gravy, cranberry sauce, stuffing and not one but two pumpkin pies! All of us dug into the box in a frenzy of feeding. Turkey was ripped off the bone, pie was being devoured at an alarming rate, and the potatoes were gone in an instant!

After about five minutes of carnage, the bird looked like buzzards picked clean some roadkill. It was an awesome display of caveman like eating. We all sat at the table and laughed. How cool was that that the hotel sent us food.

And then it happened. In walks Captain Harry, the leader of Engine Five. Now, what you have to know about this guy is, when he opens his wallet, George Washington blinks from all the sunlight. The man squeaked when he walked and had the first quarter he ever earned as a paperboy.

"Hey guys, did anyone from the Hilton bring our turkey dinner over?"

We all looked at each other. Oh no. Oops!

Shoe, our captain, said yes.

"Where is it, in the fridge?"

"Um, no, we ate it all."

"What, really funny, you assholes, now where's our dinner?"

I started cracking up! And then Pike Pole busted out laughing. Even Chief Doan started smirking.

"Sorry, Harry, the kid told us it was for us, so we were all hungry and ate it."

"You son of bitches!"

Harry and his crew stormed out of the firehouse kitchen and headed back up to Station Five, with their tails between their legs. He was mad as hell!

We all just started cracking up! We knew he was pissed and we would never hear the end of this.

The hotel manager asked the delivery kid if he knew where the firehouse was. He had grown up right by our downtown station, and said yes, he knew where it was. So that's how we ended up eating their dinner.

A simple mistake.

Captain Harry called the hotel manager and told him what had happened. The manager said they were all out of cooked turkeys and couldn't get one over to them until later. His crew finally had a turkey dinner with all the trimmings about eight o'clock that evening.

THE GHOST OF HENRY PUTT AND OTHER FIREHOUSE TALES

PLAYBOYS AND TEQUILA

My friend Pat owns Skydive Perris in Southern California, along with his sister and mom and dad. They operate a great drop zone that's one of the best in the world. I've done thousands of skydives there over the years.

I hosted an event in Belize in February 2005 that was a pretty big success. In skydiving terminology, an event like that is called a "boogie." We had skydivers from around the world join us for ten days of skydiving and SCUBA diving on Ambergris Caye. My plan was to only host one event, just for fun and to see if I could do it. Everyone had such a great time, I decided to go back again the following February. Pat asked if I wanted to use one of his Twin Otter airplanes, which holds twenty-three skydivers. We discussed it for a few days over the phone and made a deal. I announced it to the skydiving world and we had 138 people signed up in a few weeks!

About six months prior to the event I stopped in at the hangar at their airport to discuss the trip with Pat. I asked him what route we would take, as we avoided landing in Mexico the first year by going direct from Brownsville, Texas, to Belize City. Pat assured me that there would be no worries, as landing in Mexico would be easy. We would take off from Perris and fly to Loreto, Mexico, a little fishing village, and then off to Puerta Vallarta where Pat's family has a condo. Then to Oaxaca, Mexico, and Belize City, by way of overflying the thick jungles of Guatemala.

I was a little uneasy about all of the Mexico stuff. The drug wars were just getting going there, and I always had visions of some Mexican general taking our plane. Nothing like a big twin-engine aircraft with no seats, painted like a shark on the nose cone, carrying a bunch of gringos, to attract some attention.

Pat assured me there would be no issues. He said we could just bring some Playboy magazines and a bottle of tequila for the controller in the tower in Loreto. He said the guy would just lower a bucket down and we would put them in with a hundred-dollar bill and get waved right through. The control tower would send the fuel truck over and just send us right on our way. Pat said there wasn't even a customs or immigration officer at this little airport. When we got to Puerta Vallarta there would be zero trouble, as it is a big international airport and the proper paperwork would be filed. OK, I figured Pat knows what's best and it's his Twin Otter.

The next six months went by quickly. All the participants for the boogie were paid in full, and I assembled a great staff to help me with everything. There was going to be nine of us flying down with the Otter.

We took off out of Skydive Perris right before sunrise. The Otter was shaking a bit on takeoff, as we were a "bit" overweight. The Otter didn't have a heater, so we all brought really warm clothes. It gets pretty damn cold at 16,000 feet. We were going to fly about five-hour legs between fuel stops. The only thing that was worrying me now was the fact that from Loreto to Puerta Vallarta we were going to be over the Sea of Cortez with no life raft—only small inflatable devices for each of us!

My very thoughtful wife, Kristine, made us a bunch of tasty treats for the flight. It's something not one of us had even thought about! We had a cooler with about twenty giant sub sandwiches, water, Gatorade, and fruit. The Otter, besides not having any heat, only has two seats: the pilot and copilot seats. We were all sprawled out on the hard, wooden fold-down jump seats. It started to get freezing-ass cold at altitude. We were wrapped in sleeping bags and had sweatshirts and jackets on. The flight went smoothly, and we landed in Loreto after some long hours of shivering in the cold and hearing the humming propellers.

I couldn't wait to see the bribe in action.

When we landed, the control tower told us to taxi over and park next to them. So far so good. We taxied over to a designated parking area right in the shadow of the control tower. And then I saw them. Four Mexican military officers with weapons pointed at us! Pat looked a little surprised as he shut down the engines and the uniformed men approached us. While we were waiting for the engines to spool down and the

341

props to stop turning, about six more serious looking officers, with guns drawn, came out of an office at the terminal building.

I tapped Pat on the shoulder.

"Hey, Pat"

I could see he was nervous.

"What!"

"I hope you brought a lot more Playboys and tequila, I think we're gonna need them!"

"Shut the hell up!"

The Federales had us all get out of the plane at gunpoint. As we got out, we were all sweating bullets. Not just because we had guns pointed at us, but because it was about ninety degrees and we were dressed for the Arctic plane ride.

They allowed us to get out of our jackets and wanted us to unload the entire plane. Now, you can imagine how much crap we had to unload. There was all our luggage, skydive gear, tandem skydiving rigs, extra aircraft stuff, and a homemade car-battery start cart that weighed about 200 pounds.

Whenever I travel to Mexico, I always wear a fire department T-shirt. I even bring a few to give away, just in case. You see, in Mexico, firefighters are called *bomberos* and are highly respected, no matter what nation they're from. As luck would have it, the airport fire station was close to where we were parked on the tarmac. While the customs and immigration guys were going over all our paperwork, I wandered over the station.

In my broken Spanish and the *bombero* captain's broken English, I told him we were a bunch of skydivers from Los Angeles, and that I was a *bombero* there. He started smiling and called all the other firefighters out to meet me. They had just gotten a brand new "crash" rig and wanted to show it to me. They insisted I take it for a drive! I told them I had to get back to my friends, but thanked them for their hospitality and tour of their station and equipment. I went back over to the big pile of luggage sitting on the tarmac and found my backpack of clothes. I found one of my department T-shirts and headed back over to the fire station. When I gave it to the captain, he was ecstatic. I thanked him again and apologized for not having enough for the entire crew. And then it hit me! We also had six giant boxes of boogie T-shirts that had "Skydive Belize" printed on them. I ran back and dug out five boogie shirts and took them for the rest of his crew.

You would have thought I gave them a billion pesos! They thanked me over and over again. Not much probably happens during their shift, so we were a nice distraction for them. They were really great guys!

I went back to the group and we were herded inside to what seemed to be the immigration office. We had been here for about two hours already. There were all sorts of backroom discussions going on. They probably didn't know what to make of us and our unique airplane. I can only imagine what they thought was going on when they found a couple of Playboys and some booze sitting in a box!

We had been waiting in a room with no air conditioning and all of us were getting to be a mess in the heat. While the officials were trying to figure out what to do with us, in walks the fire captain. He went over to the supervisor and quietly spoke with him. The main officer, with lots of decorative medals hanging from his uniform, went over to Pat and said that was all, we were free to go.

The fire captain had come to our rescue!

However.

A couple of us had eaten half of our sandwiches Kristine had made for us and were saving the other half for the next leg of the flight. Pat got "fined" $200 US cash for "Importing meat without a proper license." Two hundred clams for half-eaten sandwiches. What a scam!

I'm sure those guys had a great night out that evening on our dime. Well, at least he had the cash ready to put in the bucket with the magazines and booze.

We loaded up the plane in the intense heat and got back on our way. We were full of fuel again and shook on takeoff. The *bomberos* all waved and smiled as we rolled down the runway. Of course, I would wait to heckle Pat until we survived the flight across the sea and were safely in a bar in Puerta Vallarta!

When we landed in Puerta Vallarta it was pretty uneventful. By the book paperwork was followed and we didn't have any guns pointed at us. I heckled Pat a little—well, maybe a *lot*—that night about his bribery scheme. What he didn't realize was that Loreto had become a popular destination and they had just renovated the entire airport. The sleepy little fishing village had grown up.

344

We took off the next day and made it to Oaxaca. There we were met by more automatic weapons in our face and were detained about an hour and a half. We had to unload the entire plane again at gunpoint. There was no fire station nearby and I think all of us were a little nervous. I mean, here we are, flying in a big turbo prop aircraft painted like a shark, saying we're all a bunch of skydivers, going to Belize. Right. No drug running going on here.

The Mexican military finally let us go without any import fines or other issues and off we went to Belize. Yes, for an inspection, we unloaded the entire plane in Belize too, just not at gunpoint.

The boogie was fantastic and we all made a lot of fun skydives over the island. We smartened up and avoided Mexico on the way home and flew from Belize to Brownsville, Texas.

It was nice to not unload the plane at gunpoint when we landed.

Adjoining Rooms, Please

A certain city fire department hockey team, that shall forever remain unnamed, was made up of some of the craziest dudes I've ever seen. They would show up at the Toronto firefighter's tournament and be the life of the party. They had wild parties every night in their hotel rooms, and I think they were drunk during every game they skated! These guys would roll into a bar and take over. They were loud, obnoxious, and funny as hell!

One year they arrived to their hotel and wanted their usual adjoining rooms. They had been staying at the same place for years, as it was close to the Woodbine horse racing track and a number of fun nightclubs and strip bars were only blocks away.

The front desk clerk told them that the connected rooms were all taken. Well, the team, after a six-hour drive, fueled by Pabst Blue Ribbon and Jack Daniels, weren't taking this very well.

Their goalie and ringleader of the team said, no problem, we'll take what you have. But we just want rooms that are next to each other.

The next morning the maid came into the room to see an unreal sight. The guys had taken a fire ax out of the hallway emergency cabinet and chopped a doorway between rooms!

There was plaster dust all over, plus beer cans and empty pizza boxes stacked high.

What a mess!

They had an early morning game and were all gone from the hotel when the carnage was discovered.

When they came back from their game, the police, who were not amused in the slightest, were there waiting for them. The teammates in the two rooms were arrested and taken away to be booked.

The team ponied up a few thousand dollars and gave it to the hotel manager, who they had known for years. They profusely apologized and begged for forgiveness. The manager actually enjoyed having them at his hotel every year, as their bar bill after a week was the total GDP of some tiny nations!

All charges were dropped and the guys were released in time for the next game.

THE NEW ROOF

As the city was growing, we went from six fire stations to eight in just a few short years. When Station Eight was built, there was something wrong with the roof. It never really kept the water out, as it was a flat type roof with only a slight slope to evacuate the rainwater. From day one it would ooze water out of the various skylights and in the corner areas. The contractor had come out a number of times to declare it fixed, only to have more rainwater soak through after every storm.

The city hired a different roofing contractor to come out and redo the entire top of the firehouse. They put on new materials in the needed areas and were there about a week. These guys seemed to really know what they were doing and it appeared they had done a great job: the leaks finally stopped.

Doctor Demerol had been promoted to captain, and was put in charge of the station maintenance. He's a great guy, but tends to get himself worked up over things a little too much sometimes. Of course, his crew took full advantage!

At Station Eight, there are eight dormitory rooms, four on each side of a long hallway with two rooms sharing one bathroom and shower. There are drop down tile ceilings with a small open space between rooms.

One evening they snuck into his dorm room and put an intravenous bag of saline water up in the ceiling and ran the plastic tubing to right above his bed. The firefighter ran the bag through the drop-down ceiling and into his room so that he could turn it on in the middle of the night and then reel it in when needed to avoid discovery.

There was a light rain that evening. Doctor Demerol climbed into his bed, ready for a good night's rest after a busy shift. About midnight the IV bag got turned on from the room next door.

Drip.

Drip.

Drip.

Drip.

And then in the dark stillness of the firehouse, the other seven firefighters heard it.

"THIS FUCKING ROOF!"

They all busted out laughing!

The IV line got quickly pulled back into the other room.

"THOSE ASSHOLES HAVEN'T FIXED SHIT!"

His door flew open as he stormed to the rig to get a big flashlight. Everyone was in their own dorm rooms, laughing their asses off.

They slowly came out, one by one to see what the ruckus was about. "Gee, Cap, what's going on? We thought the roof hasn't leaked in weeks."

He had a few of the ceiling tiles pulled down and was looking all over for the leak.

"It hasn't, but these guys had better be out here tomorrow to see what the hell is going on!"

He was really worked up.

At the morning kitchen table at shift change, he was still fuming and ranting to anyone that would listen. His crew had to finally let him in on it, before he called the deputy chief and the roofing company.

At Station Eight in the jump seat from left to right: the Viking, Jethro Bodine, Doctor Demerol, Jungle Jim, and the Grouper

THE CORNER STORE

Tommy was quite the character. He was quite the ladies' man and pretty hilarious in the locker room, on the ice, and of course, was a hit at the bars after the games. Women loved his good looks and charm.

One night we were all out at the beginning of the tournament. The bar we were in was packed and was jumping to the sound of a really entertaining band. Tommy had his eye on a young lady that was really having a fantastic time dancing the night away. He asked for her phone number and she gladly said to call her tomorrow.

After our game the next day, Tommy hit the payphone at the rink (yes, this was a while back before cell phones!) and rang her up.

They set up a dinner date for that evening. He got all dressed up and headed out that night. They had a wonderful evening and she asked if he wanted to go out again to hear a band play the following evening. Tommy said sure. So, they met up again the following evening and listened to a popular local Toronto band. Tommy tried, but he wasn't even getting to first base with this lovely woman.

She asked if he would like to come over for dinner the following evening. The week was flying by and he said sure. Even if the date didn't end up in between the sheets, a home cooked meal sure sounded better than another steak on a kaiser or chicken wings at the Steak Queen diner next to the hotel with all of us.

Tommy grabbed some wine and flowers for her and arrived at her house right on time. She had made a fantastic meal, had the mood music playing and the candles lit. Tommy just knew he was going to hit a grand slam!

After dinner and a *lot* of wine and mixed drinks, they started kissing. She asked him if he wanted to take a hot bath in her huge old-fashioned tub. Of course!

They drank another bottle of wine in the tub and she said it was time to go to bed. She asked if he had brought any condoms with him.

Damn! The one thing he didn't think of.

She said there was a corner store at the end of the block. She would just wait in the tub for him to come back. More hot water was added to the tub as he jumped out to towel off and get dressed.

It was snowing like hell outside when he left her house to run the block down to the store. He stumbled down the sidewalk, not realizing just exactly how drunk he was. He made it to the store and grabbed a pack of Trojans. His hair had frozen in the cold and he was freezing his ass off!

Tommy left the market and started staggering up the street. That's when it dawned on him. All the houses looked exactly the same on this street. They were all two-story row houses, with stone steps and small porches!

Damn, he was thinking. What house was it?

He had taken a taxi in the beginning of the evening to get there from the hotel, but couldn't remember the house number he had told the driver.

Damn! He was freezing.

He got to a house that he thought for sure was hers. He started banging on the door and tried to break into the house. He was getting frustrated as he was freezing and just wanted in!

A lady screamed at him from inside.

"Get out of here, I already called the cops!"

Damn! WRONG HOUSE.

" I've already called the cops!" she shouted again.

Damn!

Tommy bolted out off of the porch and ran down the corner and around the alley way.

There was a little neighborhood bar just off of the alley and he ducked in there to hide out and warm up.

He ordered a beer and slumped down in a corner booth.

The cops drove up and down the street a few times, flashing their spotlight around the sidewalks. He called a cab an hour later and hightailed it back to our hotel. He didn't have her phone number as he left it in his expensive leather jacket pocket, that was hanging on her dining room chair.

What a dumbass . . .

That would have been a really bad way to go: to survive a high-tension line landing, which is probably like a one in a million chance, then take a step off of the wing to a . . . splat!

The paramedics checked them both out. "Five O'clock Charlie" and his copilot didn't have a scratch on them.

Lucky bastards...

It took almost a week to get the Cessna out of the high wires.

THE VARMINT

Playing in the LEAF League was always a fun time. The games are held in the mornings on Wednesdays and Fridays. We knew most of the players in the early days of the league. There were some great battles in that era with the LA Stars, the Los Angeles County Sheriff's Department team, and we would often all go out for lunch and a few cold ones after the games. The league knew it was hard for everyone to make each game, so they allowed two civilian players on each team to help fill out the rosters.

One of our civilian players, Shawn, was an insurance salesman. He had his own business, so he could make all the games. He would show up like an NHL player, in a suit and tie, every game. His brother was a firefighter on one of the other squads, so that's how we found him. He's a pretty good player and a fun guy to have around the team.

One morning he comes rolling into our locker room in a hurry. As usual, traffic was a nightmare so he was a bit late. The rest of us were already geared up and ready to take to the ice for warm-ups. Shawn took his suit jacket and tie off and opened his gear bag.

"FUUUUUUCK!"

"AAAAGH!"

He screamed like a little school kid and jumped up onto the wooden locker room bench!

A highly irritated possum jumped up out of his gear bag and looked at all of us, bared his sharp teeth, and started hissing at everyone in the room. If you have never been around a possum, let me tell you, they can be mean little bastards. And when aggravated, they won't back down from anything or anyone!

This guy was pretty big. He bolted out of the gear bag and scrambled around the locker room in a panic. One of the guys ushered him out the door with his hockey stick, and the scared bugger ran down along the boards of the rink and disappeared.

We all had a good laugh, and Shawn's heart beat came back to somewhat normal as we took the ice for the game. He told us he had aired out his gear in his backyard the night before. The possum must have snuggled into his jersey like a down comforter for a good night's rest.

We figured the possum had run out to the back where the Zamboni was parked, getting outside through the open garage door.

Nope!

About five minutes into the game, there was a shriek from the stands. A few of the player's wives and girlfriends were running up the bleachers, with children in tow. The varmint had made its way up onto the bleacher area and was terrorizing our handful of fans!

There was a whistle to stop play on an offsides call. Everyone, including the referees were laughing, as now the Zamboni driver was chasing the possum with a broom and trash can all across the bleachers.

He finally chased it out to the Zamboni-area garage door and out he went, into the wilds of downtown Anaheim!

You're All Under Arrest, Eh!

One year we ended up in a small city in British Columbia for the firefighter's hockey tournament. The organizers put together a great event, and we had about sixty teams from all across Canada, as well as our Los Angeles team. We were hoping to do well in our division and were looking forward to seeing all our friends from the other teams.

One of the teams was notorious for raising hell and playing all sorts of pranks on other teams. They were a crazy bunch, and we usually tried to steer clear of them, as we were caught up in some of their shenanigans one year that I think will have to stay silent until I write volume three or four!

The organizers hosted a firefighter night at a local nightclub that was packed. They had advertised that firefighters from out of town would be there and that there would be a DJ, drink specials, and some raffles that evening for a local charity. It had all the makings of an incredibly entertaining evening.

When we arrived, the bar was packed! Every local young lady was there and a couple hundred firefighter hockey players.

What could possibly go wrong!

The atmosphere was electric! The DJ was killing it with the music, and the crowd on the packed dance floor was in full swing to the beat of every song played. The booze was also flowing, as were the shooters. I could sense some resentment from the locals, as they were sort of being left out by the ladies, who were paying lots of attention to all of the firefighters.

And then it happened.

SMACK!

One of the firefighters from the hell-raising team was slow dancing with a recently single lovely young lady. Her ex-boyfriend couldn't take it any longer and went out on the dance floor and punched the firefighter right in the nose, knocking him to the floor unconscious and bleeding.

Well, you can only imagine what happened next!

His teammates pounced on the guy and the ten or so bouncers got involved quickly to keep a full-on brawl from breaking out! The security team did a great job of clearing the mayhem to the outside. A couple of scuffles broke out between some firefighters and locals, but nothing serious erupted.

When the ambulance arrived, they started working on the injured lover boy, but his teammates wanted to treat his injuries. They pushed the two ambulance attendants aside and worked on him themselves. They loaded him up on the gurney and wheeled him to the ambulance.

"OK, you guys, you treated him, now let me and my partner take him to the hospital." The ambulance medic pleaded.

They pushed the two paramedics out of the way again and jumped in the ambulance. "We got it, now one of you get in and show me where the hospital is!"

One of the paramedics got in, while the other was just standing there in the night club parking lot, wondering where the police were! The ambulance peeled out of the parking lot, jumping a curb to miss some vehicles.

It was a busy night for the Royal Canadian Mounted Police (RCMP) that evening; they didn't have anyone to immediately speed to a broken-up bar fight. Just as the ambulance sped away down the highway, a Mountie arrived. When the ambulance paramedic told him what happened, he radioed dispatch and took off after it, with the ambulance driver riding shotgun.

When the ambulance arrived at the hospital, there were a couple of RCMP vehicles waiting for them in the emergency room parking lot. When they got out to wheel in their buddy, they got the news . . .

"You're all under arrest, eh!"

The ER staff came out and helped wheel in their friend. All of them were handcuffed and put into the patrol cars. And you're all charged with

hampering an emergency worker in the line of duty,

kidnapping,

theft,

disorderly conduct,

bodily harm,

and, of course, a pending DUI with the blood result.

The RCMP Mounties, they always get their man!

The teammates spent the night in the pokey, and their injured friend spent the night in the hospital for observation. Luckily, it was just a broken nose and a minor concussion. Half the guys that played in the tournament were suffering from that!

The event organizers were notified of the situation and in the morning let their fire chief know what had happened. They were pretty pissed that something like this went down. A peace summit was arranged with the commander of the RCMP at the police headquarters.

It turns out the teammate that drove the ambulance hadn't been drinking, as he was their designated driver for the evening, and the other players, who had been hitting it hard that night, were very apologetic. Details of the deal have been kept sealed for years, but I think a very sizable donation was made to the RCMP formal dance and fundraiser event. And a sincere apology, some Tim Hortons coffee, and donut money were given to the ambulance crew.

The RCMP commander, the fire chief, and tournament organizers really chewed their asses, banishing them from the tournament for a few years.

THE DANIEL ORTEGA CHRONICLES (YES, *THAT* DANIEL ORTEGA!)

One

During my time hosting the skydiving boogies down in Belize, I ended up working with one of the most over the top, fun, craziest people you could ever meet: Miss Rosalie.

Rosalie had a TV talk show in Belize. She covered all sorts of subjects and was pretty well connected to some of the government officials. Rosalie was quite the "character," you could say. Her show was on a couple Sundays per month, and she seemed to know everyone in Belize.

I met her through my friends, Andy and Antoinette. Andy is an old-time jumper from Texas that has lived in Belize for years now. We met right before I hosted the first boogie there in 2005; he had called me up, hearing I was bringing skydiving to Belize.

Andy, and at the time Colin, a Scotsman in the British military based in Belize, were the only two licensed jumpers in the nation. Both were well connected to the Belize Defense Force (BDF) Air Wing, formerly commanded by our pal Lieutenant Colonel Ganney Dortch. Ganney would get a lot of his clothes from Andy and Antoinette's clothing store and would go out of his way to help us with our skydiving logistics.

Every so often we would get to jump out of the BDF Defender aircraft for an exhibition jump into either downtown Belize City into one of the soccer fields or the Belize Zoo.

One day I get a phone call from an excited Rosalie. The government was hosting a giant Independence Day rally in downtown Belize City and wanted to know if we could skydive in with the official flag of Belize.

The Governor General of Belize, Sir Colville Young, was also hosting a big reception the evening of the jump. Rosalie figured it was a good time for me to meet a bunch of the Belizean movers and shakers, including the prime minister.

I agreed to come down to perform the jump, as Belize had become like a second home to me and my family over the years. And what an honor to be asked to jump in with the official ceremonial flag flying behind me in front of a huge crowd.

Andy met me at the international airport. He had arranged everything for the jump, securing the BDF aircraft and other prejump issues. Another friend of ours, Tom, owned a house out on Ambergris Caye, so he was going to jump with us too.

Andy took us down to look at our designated landing area. Like most cities, Belize City is a very densely populated area with buildings, power lines, and an assortment of other very bad things for a skydiver to run in to. The city is at the edge of the Caribbean Sea.

There's a street that was next to the sea wall to land on. Big bleachers were set up in front of the Memorial Park to handle the anticipated large crowd. There would be thousands of people there for the Independence Day festivities. The plan was for us to jump in with the flag, then they were going to raise it on the big flagpole in the middle of the park.

We had one shot at this and no time to do a practice jump. At least the road was next to the ocean, the way the wind usually comes in, so there would be no buildings to cause "rotors," an air disturbance that is havoc on parachutes.

Our designated landing area was tight. We had about 200 feet of paved road to land on, or get wet in the sea or zapped by power lines. The last thing we wanted to do was die an agonizing death in front of thousands of cheering fans! We carefully reviewed all our options and came up with a pattern to fly for a great show.

Andy said he wasn't current enough to feel comfortable landing there, as he hadn't jumped in a few months. Colin and Tom were cool with it, and no way was I backing out. It really wasn't too tough of a gig, but it's always nerve-racking to do a demo jump in front of an entire nation on national television and thousands of spectators. We went over the plan one more time together.

On the day of the show we went back to the landing area. It's always my personal policy to check one final time on jump day, as we don't want to be surprised by something parked in the middle of the LZ after getting out of the plane. One year I had done a jump with Andy onto a soccer field in downtown Belize City that they had parked two helicopters on between the time we checked it and the time we got out of the plane! We had to fly in and land between the parked helicopters main rotor blades!

All was good at the landing area, so we went over to the BDF Air Wing base and met with Ganney. We reviewed our aircraft jump-run heading for an exit to put us in the right opening spot and a timing plan, as we were supposed to get out on cue at a certain time to land on the target.

Show time . . .

We double checked our skydiving gear and I rechecked the flag bag I was carrying. It was a canvas bag that was secured to my chest strap, held closed with Velcro. The last thing I wanted to do was lose it on exit! As we were taxiing out to the runway at the international airport, in flies a big Antonov Russian-made airliner. I squinted to see what was on the tail insignia. Is that a Nicaraguan flag? Who would be in that thing?

We got in our slot to take off between the Antonov landing, plus a few of the local planes arriving and departing. We took off and headed the couple miles into the city, climbing slowly to our exit altitude.

And naturally, it started raining.

The show must go on!

We got to our exit altitude of 5,000 feet and flew around waiting for our cue to jump. As many of you probably know, Central American time isn't exactly like Swiss railway time!

We flew around for about thirty minutes, checking out the giant crowd at the park and laughing about how small that street we were about to land on looked, as rain drops spit in through the open door.

The rain clouds finally parted to a gorgeous day. The sea looked magnificent in her green and blue hues, reflecting the sunlight off the small swells coming in slowly. We could see out to the various islands and into the mainland for miles and miles. It was now a perfect day for a skydive.

We got our cue to jump!

Tom and Colin jumped first and then I exited. I had a nice, soft opening of my parachute and opened my chest mounted flag bag to unfurl and fly the official colors of Belize.

I almost dropped the damn thing as I took it out of the bag! That would have been pretty embarrassing. I hooked the flag up to fly behind me and started to concentrate on the landing.

Flying high above the ocean, I was enjoying the sight of the city from high above. The Caribbean Sea was now a solid emerald green; I could see for miles in all directions.

Slowly turning to lose altitude and stay close to the landing area, I followed Tom and Colin in to land. Tom gently touched down first and then Colin, as we had planned. All the military members were saluting the flag as it flew in.

Perfect!

A perfect landing while the Belize national anthem was playing.

As I set down to a nice soft landing and grabbing the national flag so it wouldn't touch the ground, a well-dressed man in the crowd, surrounded by a bunch of dark suit-and-tie guys, was screaming his approval in Spanish.

Is that Daniel Ortega? I had to do a quick double take.

Yup!

He was waving his hands about and screaming in Spanish and smiling. I gave him a smile and then turned to hand the flag to the minister of tourism, so he could then hand it to the prime minister to raise on the park's giant flag pole. Ortega was still cheering along with all of the onlookers!

They raised the flag while the Belize national anthem was played. It was a pretty cool sight, as all of the military members were saluting and every Belizean was so proud at that moment. Belize is a very young nation, gaining independence from Britain on September 21, 1981.

I high fived Tom and Colin and we came to the consensus we really needed a beer. Andy and Antoinette were our ground crew and already had the bar at the Radisson Hotel picked out.

Colin had biffed his landing a bit and scuffed up his hand on the sidewalk. As the medical professional I am, I ordered him to clean the wound and drink two Belikin beers, stat! Being the good soldier, he was more than happy to follow my orders, but actually had four or five.

I asked Andy if he knew Ortega was flying in. He said it was a last-minute deal and they let him give this rousing speech, entirely in Spanish, after Prime Minister Musa had spoken.

I started laughing and said no way George W. Bush was letting me back in to the USA!

That evening I actually put a suit and tie on for the first time in forever and went to the Governor General's reception with Rosalie. It was a great event. Everyone wanted to talk about skydiving, and I met with the Prime Minister and a host of other important people in the Belizean government. I spent a lot of time with the ambassadors from Cuba and Venezuela. I told my Angel Falls story and the Venezuelan ambassador personally invited me to go back there with him some day. I was really hoping Ortega was going to be there, but he flew back to Nicaragua after his speech that afternoon.

I was a *long* way from that gravel road in Ohio. What an interesting evening!

Unfortunately, both Rosalie Staines and Andy's wife, Antoinette, recently passed away after short illnesses. They were both a lot of fun to be around.

Two

After eight events in seven years, progress started to infringe upon our landing area in Belize. The first year it was such a wide-open area, but condominium development really shortened our landing area into an unsafe area to host a boogie.

I was looking for a new spot and one day on Google Earth I found a hotel and runway in Nicaragua that looked perfect. The Nicaraguans had wanted me to bring the skydivers there for a few years, as they were really ramping up their tourism industry.

I called Sharon, who worked for a big Los Angeles public-relations firm that represented Nicaragua. We had spoken before, and I figured she would be all in if it was possible to move the boogie.

Sharon was really happy I called and set the wheels in motion. INTUR is the tourism department for Nicaragua. They were excited at a new activity and agreed to fly myself and my wife, Kristine, down for an official meeting. We found someone to watch our two ankle biters and flew down on Memorial Day weekend. We didn't know what to expect but agreed it was going to be an adventure!

We were greeted by a woman that had a sign with our names on it at the Managua Airport. We only had two carry-ons with us, so off we went to the "official" car. A beat-up old Toyota pickup with no working air conditioning. We weaved through the Managua traffic and pulled into the INTUR office. There we met Julio, the number two official in the office, behind the minister of tourism, Mr. Salinas.

We were welcomed like movie stars at their office. Julio is an energetic guy and was incredibly excited about the prospect of skydivers coming to Nicaragua.

We met Mr. Salinas, who was very excited also. I told them both my Belize Daniel Ortega story and they loved it. They spoke about how they were trying to bring more tourism to Nicaragua, laid out some of their ideas and listened intently as I informed them about what was needed for a successful skydiving event.

No one from outside of the country had ever done a legal jump there (the CIA did ops during Iran-Contra). They were going to work closely with the civil aviation department called INAC to get all of the approvals we would need.

Kristine and I had a fun weekend. We checked out the resort and runway and laid the ground work for the boogie. Before we returned to the states, we had a final meeting with Julio and sorted out a few things that would be a necessity, like a fuel truck, as the airport we were going to use didn't have any fuel storage tanks.

All systems were a go! It was a very productive three-day, whirlwind trip.

A few months later I receive a phone call from a very excited Julio. There's a big river festival in San Carlos, Nicaragua, every year. It's right on the river that divides Nicaragua and Costa Rica on the eastern side of the nation. The festival is a huge party, with all sorts of party boats and floats. There's live music, ethnic foods, and *lots* of cold beer!

Julio wanted to know if I could come down with another jumper and skydive out of a helicopter into the party.

"Yes—no—HELL YES!"

The plan was for us to fly down and tour the country for eleven days. We would have a driver and a tour guide. They wanted to take us to Granada, León, and the Cerro Negro Volcano that you can sand board down. It was all for me to see what the skydiving group would want to do while they were in Nicaragua, and also to meet with tour guides and other industry stakeholders. We would also meet with civil aviation officials and the commander of the Nicaraguan military airborne division.

I got on the phone and called Lyal up, my brother from another mother. He runs a drop zone, Skydive Eden North, west of Edmonton, Canada, and had been helping me with all my boogies. When I told him the plan, that we were going to Nicaragua in October, he just laughed. Of course, he was in!

I flew out of San Diego and Lyal took off out of Edmonton. We met in Houston for our connection to Managua. We really didn't know what we were getting ourselves in to, but we knew it was going to be a quite an adventure,

Our driver for the entire time, Tomas, met us at the Managua airport. Tomas is one of the best human beings I've ever met. He spoke little English, but over the time we were there, became friends with us.

Tomas took us to the INTUR office where we met with Julio. They had a nice hotel for us to stay in for two nights in the city, as we had to meet with Lt. Colonel Aguirre, the commander of the Nicaragua military paratroopers and then later with the civil aviation department called INAC.

The next day we met with the colonel. He was a somewhat serious man but smiled as we told of our skydiving experience and qualifications. He was there to see if we actually knew what we were doing. After Lyal and I spoke with him a while, and we discussed the Russian military gear his men jump, he just shook our hands and said it was an honor to have us be there to skydive.

He told Julio that we knew what we were doing and to roll out the red carpet for us.

After that meeting, we had to visit with the INAC team. These fellows weren't too sure about letting us jump out of a perfectly good helicopter. They were really nervous about all of it. We drove out to the international airport and met them in their office.

We took our skydiving gear, and they had the Robinson R-44 helicopter, a four-seater, meet us. It was the pilot and ship we were supposed to jump out of in a week. Aviation, like skydiving, is a small world, I knew the instructors that the pilot had gotten his commercial ticket from in Long Beach. We knew about twenty of the same people, so that put the pilot at ease right away.

The aviation inspectors took photos of us getting in and out of the bird with our rigs on. Then they wanted photos of all our gear, asking all sorts of questions. Wow, they were nervous about everything. We went back to their office and discussed everything they would need from me for an event, and what I would expect from them. They started warming up to the idea of having 200 hundred skydivers come to Nicaragua. They also were on board with us jumping from the helicopter for the river festival.

We left the airport and went back to meet with Julio at his tourism office. The inspectors from INAC had called him already and given their approval for us to jump.

We met Freddy, who was going to be our tour guide for the entire trip, and jumped in with Tomas in his four-seat pickup to start touring Nicaragua. Freddy worked for one of the large tour companies and was knowledgeable about all things Nicaragua. We had a few days to explore before the exhibition jump, so we went to Granada for a couple of days and then up to León. It was a great experience as Freddy would tell us stories of Nicaragua, all about the Iran-Contra era, and the history of how Ortega came to power.

It was fascinating.

I didn't really know what to expect on this trip. Part of me was a bit worried, as like everyone, I had seen the images from the Reagan-era Iran-Contra ordeal and had visions that Nicaragua was a violent place. What Lyal and I encountered was the complete opposite of what we expected. I had been there only for a few days with Kristine, so we really didn't get to see the countryside like this. Everywhere we went, the Nicaraguan people were so kind to us. They would laugh and help us with our pitiful Spanish, but encouraged us to keep trying to speak it. Many had questions about America and Canada and wanted to know what brought us to Nicaragua. It's a very poor nation, and I don't want to get into politics in a book about fun and adventure, but I felt for the people there that work so hard to get by, all smiling as they go. The amazing folks we met along our travels deserve a better government and representation. However, I guess you could say that about a lot of places these days.

We had to drive back through Managua on our way to San Carlos from León. It was going to be a very long drive down the east side of Lake Nicaragua. Driving in Central America means kids on bikes, motorcycles, cows, horses, baby strollers, and broken-down vehicles, many without headlights. And the pot holes. Wow! I thought I was back in Pennsylvania.

One of the coolest street people I've ever seen was a young girl about twelve or thirteen juggling in the middle of a busy intersection in Managua. She was so incredible and was throwing them so high, not dropping a single one. We quickly dug out some money for her. Lyal tried to get her performance captured on his GoPro, but it was brand new and I don't think the old timer knew how it worked!

We pulled into San Carlos on Friday afternoon. It was a hell of a long, beautiful drive, but we were ready for a beer. The town is on a hillside, and in the little downtown area there are a lot of bars and restaurants overlooking the park and river.

Julio was there waiting for us with a crowd of famous Nicaraguan TV personalities. The restaurant we were in was elbow to elbow with people—the weekend party was in full swing. The plan was for us to jump at midday into the downtown park. We couldn't wait!

Julio had this odd look on his face when we were discussing the details of the jump. He took me and Lyal aside.

"Hey guys, we have a problem"

"What?"

"The civil aviation inspectors have scrubbed your jump from the helicopter and won't allow it."

Well, I said quite a few choice words and asked Julio how we can get it approved.

"We have a phone call in to the first lady. The minister is very good friends with her and he has explained the situation"

Just then it dawns on me.

"Julio, remember the story I told you and Minister Salinas, call her and have her ask her husband about the time he saw the person skydiving in Belize, tell him that skydiver is here to jump in his country now!"

Julio lit up. He grabbed his phone and called Mr. Salinas. After a very animated conversation, he hung up.

"We'll see if it works."

I told Lyal no way in hell were we going to jump in the morning. We consumed a lot of Flor de Caña rum that night, drowning our sorrows.

When Tomas took us over to our hotel, it was a little shack of a place at the end of a dirt road. Chickens were running around and there was a giant pig buried in the mud just outside of our room. He made a racket all night! The experiences on this trip were just getting better, and funnier.

About 8 a.m. there was a loud banging on my door. It was Freddy our tour guide. "Mr. Rich, Mr. Lyal, she said yes, she said yes! The jump is *on*. Get up!"

Freddy kept shouting at us! I opened the door and Lyal came into my room. Freddy said that the first lady had ordered civil aviation to allow us to jump, because her husband remembered my performance in Belize.

Classic!

The helicopter was now on its way from Managua. We went down to the park where they had wanted us to land. We moved around a bunch of giant wooden-horse carvings they had for decorative props and cleared a landing area in front of the giant stage the various bands were to perform on. We both had our sport parachutes with us, nothing that we could set down easy, like an accuracy jump. These parachutes needed some distance to land. We measured out our landing area and decided to do a practice jump to see if we could shut our canopies down for landing in the short runway we had in front of the stage.

The helicopter arrived with a couple of the INAC inspectors on board. They were still looking nervous. We told them the plan about doing a practice jump. They liked that idea and wanted to see a jump in person before we were cleared for the exhibition skydive. We boarded the helicopter after briefing the pilot. He took us up to about 4,000 feet above the ground and over the airport.

It's always fun to jump from a helicopter, but this jump was even more special and the view was amazing! I followed Lyal around as we descended to our measured-out landing area in the grass next to the runway.

We both got our parachutes stopped in the distance we needed; however, we decided to have our own safety meeting on this. We decided that we could most likely land in the middle of the park, surrounded by thousands of people.

However.

It was about a seven-hour drive there from Managua: we figured even just a broken ankle was going to be a really, really bad ordeal. In our "younger days" we would have just done it. But hey, we were in our fifties now . . . and if we broke a hip at our age . . .! We both decided the juice wasn't worth the squeeze.

The aviation inspectors were already not at all at ease with this and if one of us died a spectacular death in front of thousands of partygoers, the boogie would get cancelled!

We told the inspectors we would land at the airport in the giant grass area instead of in the middle of the crowd in front of the stage. They smiled in relief. The airport was only about a half a mile up the hill from the downtown party site and river, so the crowd could see us easily if we went higher and exited over them, allowing time to make a run back to the airport under canopy. We had to time it right though, as there was nothing but trees, houses, and power lines on that half a mile.

A couple of hours later was now showtime. We got in the helicopter and took off from the airport, standing outside with one foot on the skids, waving to the crowd as we flew above the party. Of course, it started sprinkling a little rain—but after all we had to go through, no way in hell were we not jumping today!

The crowd went crazy waving at us. We orbited above them and climbed to about 7,000 feet. As the pilot put us into a hover, we carefully climbed out onto the skids and gave the count. One, two, three and off we went, falling off backwards, accelerating through the air for about 1,000 feet until we deployed our parachutes. I was a little lower than Lyal as planned. The crowd was going crazy! None of them had ever seen a *paracaidista* before in person. The Spanish word for skydiver.

Lyal flew over and top docked on my canopy. (For you non jumpers, it means he hooked his feet into the front lines of my parachute and we flew hooked together.) We maneuvered around high overhead as the crowd was gasping and screaming. I guess they thought we had accidently wrapped up our parachutes!

At about 2,000 feet, we broke off and flew separately back toward the airport. The INAC inspectors were there clapping for us and smiling. I could see they were relieved; I knew that they would have been in serious trouble with their boss if we were injured.

When we landed, Tomas had the truck waiting. We jumped in the back, still with our gear on and opened parachutes in hand as he drove us quickly down to the crowd.

As we ran into the park area, in front of a huge crowd of people cheering, I was pretty happy and proud.

We actually pulled it off.

The first two gringos to jump "legally" in Nicaragua.

We high fived all the kids, and they all wanted to touch our parachutes. There were a bunch of huge boats out on the river with bands playing rock and roll, and hundreds of people dancing on each boat.

It was a surreal scene. What a party!

Later that day we went up to the old San Carlos Fort for dinner. We met with Julio and Minister Salinas. They introduced us to many different dignitaries, and we learned more about the country.

It was amazing.

Not bad for a kid from a gravel road in Ohio and a Canadian kid from a farm in Onoway, Alberta!

And, we had the Ortega's permission for the boogie.

The following February we arrived with 205 people in tow for the event. It was very windy that week so we didn't skydive much. However, the skydivers toured all around the country and had a memorable time.

I've now hosted international skydiving events in Belize, Nicaragua, Palau, Maldives, and Costa Rica. The worldview I've gained from these experiences is like getting a master's degree in humanity. My wife and I fell in love with all these magical places, and now live full time in Costa Rica, but I still need help with my Spanish.

Go travel, it's good for your mind and soul.

My Best (or Worst) Screwups!

Slowdown! If it's burning when they call us,
it will be burning when we get there.

—Red

It's been a lot of fun writing about all these things that have happened over the years. Writing this book has brought back some really great memories of fantastic people and adventures. So, you might be wondering about my mishaps on the job, besides of course getting on the wrong fire truck as a sixteen-year-old volunteer firefighter one night, and putting the Magic Blanket on a dead man that came back to life!

Everyone in the fire service at some point in their career does something incredibly dumb. Maybe even a couple of things. One of my favorite battalion chiefs got the name Hose Clamp Eddie, because, at a fully involved house fire, he opened the hose clamp on the supply line from the fire hydrant to the pumper before it was unhooked, thus charging 1,600 feet of four-inch fire hose in the hose bed! Things like that happen to the best of us.

Pull the Right Handle!

We had a pretty bad medical emergency call, so we had to do patient follow up to the hospital because the ambulance crew needed our paramedic to assist them in the ambulance. I had to move up from the jump seat and drive, as it was our engineer that was the medic that went to the hospital in the back of the ambulance. The hospital was in the next town over, covered by a different city fire department. As we approached the hospital, I could see a plume of very thick black smoke coming from behind the emergency room driveway. As we pulled in, we saw what was burning: a doctor's new Mercedes was fully involved!

I parked the pumper and put it in "pump," a handle that needs to be engaged to make the pump run when the apparatus is stopped. The firefighter jumped off and pulled the hose reel to get a quick knock down. I pulled the wrong handle on the pump panel and charged the preconnected line in the cross lay bed! It quickly filled with 150 psi of tank water.

Damn!

And, of course, the neighboring department had just arrived and witnessed my screw up. No hiding from that one!

Slow Down!

When I worked in Pennsylvania, I learned a good lesson about driving to a call too fast. (As Red always said, if it's burning when they call us, it'll be burning when we get there.)

There was an apartment building on fire and it was at the unit of one of the city council members. It was reported by their neighbors that he and his wife were trapped inside. I was driving the ladder truck that day, and it wouldn't fire up right away. The pumper sped off without me. I finally got it fired up and took off out of the firehouse to a light rain that had made the streets pretty slick. As I got to an intersection, a car pulled out in front of me and I ended up standing on the brakes! The giant ladder truck slid sideways and I barely got it under control before almost hitting the power pole on the sidewalk! My heart was in my throat and I could just imagine explaining to Old Dad how I totaled the apparatus. When I got there, fire was blowing out of the front door and the windows. We did a quick knock down and went in to search the apartment to no avail. Luckily, they weren't home that afternoon.

Lesson learned!

You Hit What?

After that, in all the years of driving apparatus of all types, the only thing I ever hit was a curb, except . . .

The dumbest thing I ever did was to drive the basket of our old ladder truck into our brand-new fire station. Yes, you read that right! I ran the basket of the ladder truck right into a shiny new steel roll-up door at a whopping one mile per hour!

We had taken the ladder truck out for a spin, as it was our reserve unit and didn't get much use. It was an old Van Pelt model from the 1970s, rear mounted with the basket hanging out over the cab. It had seen a *lot* of action over the years and was getting a little worn out. The basket obscured a lot of vision from the driver's seat. As we were pulling back in, Jethro Bodine was backing in Big Foot, our off-road giant water tender brush rig. His bay door was all the way up, and I had seen ours go up also. As I was pulling in, he started honking Big Foot's air horn like crazy!

And then, at barely moving, I suddenly stopped and saw some broken plastic float to the ground in front of me.

Damn.

I just ran the basket into the bottom two inches of the roll-up door that wasn't quite all the way up yet! And to make matters even worse, there was our chief, Hose Clamp Eddie, watching the entire mishap from ten feet away! Well, there's nothing quite like smashing a fire truck into the firehouse in front of your chief. I guess that takes some skill.

What a dumbass.

I set the air brake and got out to assess the damage. The door had a small crinkle in it and was off the tracks on both sides. The basket had some minor damage to it. The reflector lights are what shattered, and one of the leveling arms, sort of like a shock absorber, was broken at the connector. Bodine came over to me and asked why I didn't stop when he was honking at me. How the hell did I know that's what he was trying to tell me! The chief helped assess the damage and said it was just a dumb accident. The captain wanted me to be written up, but luckily for me, he was shot down by the chief. I told the chief I thought United Airlines must have been flying over and stopped the door from going up during a call to the tower!

"Good one, Reaper!" He was the same chief that handled the Station Four debacle with the door.

Pete our longtime department mechanic that could fix anything came by to check things out. He said it wasn't a big deal to fix, but he wanted to remove the basket for a long time. He worked on it in his spare time at his shop for a month and removed the basket so it was now just a straight ladder. He cut off the basket control box and gave it to me for a souvenir. We ended up sending the old Van Pelt to our sister city in Mexico about a year later.

Every single time I drove in or out of the station after that afternoon, I made sure, no matter what I was driving, that the door was all the way up!

There are probably about twenty more stories of my screwups that former coworkers will be sending me after reading this book. I'll save those for volume two!

Oh yeah, I also scored on Spence, our own LA Blazers goalie, two different times trying to clear the puck out of our own zone.

What a dumbass!

CHRISTINE THE TRUCK!

Remember the 1983 Stephen King horror movie about the possessed car named Christine? This story is about a pickup truck that thought it was Christine!

The crew from Station Three was called to a vehicle accident. A pickup truck had rammed into a car at a busy intersection. The driver of the truck was reported to be pinned under the steering wheel, so the captain on Engine Three called for Truck One to roll because it has all of the vehicle extrication tools on it.

When Engine Three arrived, there was a car spun out onto the sidewalk and the pickup sitting in the middle of the street, with a badly damaged front end and steam shooting out of the smashed radiator. The driver was pinned under the steering wheel and both doors were jammed shut from the impact. Not a problem, as the truckers will arrive and make mincemeat out of this pickup in minutes by popping the doors, removing the roof, and pulling the steering wheel back with the hydraulic tools. This is so routine; most firefighters can do it in their sleep!

Hop jumped in the bed of the pickup, holding cervical spine immobilization and putting a C-collar on the driver through the back slider window. The Bhagwan crawled in through the side window and started working up the driver. The captain and other paramedic went to work on the driver of the car. This call was going like clockwork. The truck company arrived and the crew started setting up the extrication tools just as two ambulances arrived. A call like this happens every few minutes across the globe.

Again. It's as routine as routine gets.

Well.

Bhagwan got an IV started on the driver, a male about fifty years old. The truck company started prying the driver's side door open with the spreader tool when all of a sudden—

Vroooooooooooooooooooooooom!

The pickup started all by itself!

It was in gear, so it lurched forward, peeling rubber as it started to head down the street! A police officer measuring the skid marks had to jump out of the way and was just barely missed. Hop held on to the driver, as he was holding on to him through the window and had nothing else to really grab on to! Bhagwan was frantically trying to steer, but couldn't because the wheel was pressed too strongly into the driver's stomach to turn it!

Off they went down the street for about a hundred feet, heading towards a power pole. Hop was holding on to the driver for dear life as the pole rapidly approached! Bhagwan braced himself inside with the driver.

BLAM!

Right into a utility pole head on. Bhagwan went headfirst into the dashboard, and Hop went body first into the cab. The power spreaders were still stuck in the door and the vehicle dragged the spreaders, hydraulic lines, and power unit along with it, bouncing down the street! The truck company crew just watched in amazement! It's all they could do.

What a mess!

Luckily, no one was injured besides a few bumps, and the driver wasn't injured any more than he already was. This truck was truly possessed: no one could remember that ever happening. The truck company inspected the tools and went right back to work, quickly getting the patient removed from the vehicle. Of course, after cutting the battery cables. Hop actually kept the driver's head in place during the crash. It's probably the only thing that kept him from a broken neck.

Afterward, the crews huddled together to figure out what had happened. Why did this truck just start up and start motoring? We always had a policy to cut the battery cables at car accidents, but this pickup was so smashed up in the front, nobody thought about the battery disconnect being necessary. I can guarantee that every single car accident after that day, lots of damage or a fender bender, had the cables removed or cut!

Spoons!

O ne of the all-time best pranks at the hockey tournaments was a game we called Spoons. If you do an internet search, there are some great examples of how it's done.

We would find a Canadian team that we knew well to see if they had any gullible, rough and tumble rookies. Every year we would find a new player that was full of piss and vinegar, wanting to show his toughness to the crowd. After a few shots of Kamikazes for said rookie, we would pit him in a spoons battle against our Los Angeles world champion, usually Doak, the biggest player on our team. We would get two big tablespoons and wrap hockey tape around the handles. This was to "protect" their teeth.

The spoons game was always hosted at a crowded bar or at the hotel hospitality room, in front of many of the other teams. We would put a tape line on the floor and gather the crowd around. There would be introductions, like a heavyweight boxing match. One of the best rookies we ever got to play along was self-titled with the nickname of Razor: a big, strong Canadian kid.

His teammates pumped him up to take on the American champ and to, under no circumstances, ever give up until a win. We pumped a few more beers into him and egged him on, telling him no one had defeated Doak in years!

Doak and Razor took to the floor on their hands and knees, opposite each other. Hands behind the tape line. I was the "referee." The object is to put the spoon in your mouth and whack your opponent on the head with it, taking turns, until the first one to give up loses.

Now, you're reading this and thinking, "How the hell can you whack someone hard with a table spoon in your mouth?"

Well, you can't! That's where the "referee" comes in! I had a big soup spoon hidden in my back pocket. As Razor went down on his hands and knees to allow Doak to whack him, I would pull the spoon out, look at the crowd, put my finger to my lips so that the crowd would stay quiet, and hit him on the noggin.

Whack!

This went on for quite a while, as a young, mighty Razor was determined not to lose to a Yank!

Finally, after hitting him about thirty times, I officially declared the match a draw.

Cheers erupted from the crowd, as most everyone was dying laughing!

"RAZOR! RAZOR! RAZOR!" the crowd chanted his name.

We congratulated Razor and told him he was a stud, then I asked him to whack Doak one final time. As he went to hit him, spoon in mouth, I pulled out my spoon from my back pocket and he watched as I smacked Doak on the head. The place went crazy with laughter! Razor realized he had been gotten by the best. He just shook his head and was mobbed by his teammates.

The next day on the ice, we stopped in to watch his game. His helmet wasn't fitting so well due to the knots on his noggin! Razor became an instant legend on his department that night.

We pulled this on a lot of players from many different teams over the years.

What a classic!

GOODBYE, LINCOLN STREET

M om was tired of cleaning such a big house and Dad was tired of yard work. Even after he did buy that riding lawn mower the week before I moved out after high school!

He built the house in 1964. It was a split level with four floors and the apartment in the basement for my grandma. She had passed away, so it became just way too much house for them. They had loved the neighbors and everything about the house, but it was time.

Our house was like the neighborhood emergency room when I was growing up. My dad was on the volunteer fire department and had lots of first-aid training. Kids were always showing up with cuts, BBs stuck in them from air rifle wars in the woods, broken arms and legs, and other assorted kid injuries. We had a medicine cabinet stocked with all sorts of bandages and the 1970s cure all, the red chemical Mercurochrome.

One day Butchie, a neighbor a few years older than I, who my dad always said was going to kill himself on his dirt bike, did a fantastic wheelie up Lincoln Street, then proceeded to do one at full speed on the downhill end. He lost control on the gravel and flew head first into the ditch. Luckily, my dad was home and he heard the crash.

Now, there was an ambulance of sorts in our town, run by the local funeral home. They outfitted the hearse with some medical supplies when it wasn't taking folks for their final ride to the local cemetery. I always teased the owner that he would drive people slow to the hospital if they were doing poorly so he could bill for the ride and the funeral! So instead of waiting for the ambulance, we held Butchie still and my dad found a piece of plywood from our garage. We taped his head down and his body, plus held towels on his gaping open leg wound that was really bleeding all over. A neighbor stopped in his station wagon. We loaded Butchie up and off he went to the hospital emergency room in the back of the Pontiac wagon.

In that era, the doctors didn't even blink when they saw a high-school kid strapped to a sheet of plywood carried into the ER. My dad went along to hold traction on his neck and to keep the towel on his leg so that he didn't bleed out. The staff thanked my dad for doing such a great job of packaging him up to get him in one piece to the ER. I think Butchie's family sent us a ham for saving their Evel Knievel wannabe son.

Our long-time next-door neighbors, Paul and Gen Bender, had sold their house to move to a condo. They were stalwarts on the street and my folks were sad to see them go. Mrs. Bender and my mom would drink coffee nearly every morning together and discuss Johnny Carson's monologue from the previous night, while puffing away on their cigarettes. They were wonderful friends, more like family, really. But their kids had also grown up and moved on, so they also wanted to downsize.

The family that bought their house had some small children, and my mom was excited to have kids playing again, as all of us had grown and moved away from the surrounding homes. The new people weren't very friendly, and to this day I couldn't tell you what their names are. And that might happen in a big city, but not on our rural little gravel road. Mom took them a pie as a welcoming gift, and they just thanked her and slammed the door in her face.

Jimmy grew up in the house on the other side of the Benders. He was quite the wild kid growing up. One evening we were having dinner, and a four-year-old Jimmy, being chased by his dad, Big Jim, ran naked through our back yard! We all just laughed and kept eating dinner. It seems he didn't want a bath that evening.

Little Jim was a handful. There was a big oak tree in their yard and Jimmy would climb this thing every day. His dad told him not to do it. Big Jim would come home from working all night at the mill and go to sleep. We would try to play quietly on those afternoons so he could get some rest. We all loved Big Jim. He was one of those guys that could fix anything. He also had a little A-framed shop in his back yard. It was adorned with Playboy centerfolds, so we always went over to help hold a screwdriver or wrench for him! Big Jim also liked his cold beer, and we would get a sip now and then.

Well, one day, Jimmy decides to climb the tree. Big Jim had just gotten home from the mill and was already fast asleep.

Well, of course, that afternoon, Jimmy fell out and broke his arm!

Big Jim heard the crying and came outside to see what had happened. Man, was he pissed off, as I also ran out when we heard Jimmy's shrieks of pain to see what was going on.

"Jimmy, I told you not to climb this tree"!

Whack!

He gave Jimmy one swift crack with his belt, not at all hard, but just for effect. He had told Jimmy to never climb the tree. Over and over. We wrapped up his arm in a pillow and his mom drove him to the hospital to get fixed up.

I can only imagine in today's world that would be on a cell phone video somewhere and go viral. But I can guarantee you this much . . . Jimmy would get the shakes if anyone dared him to climb that oak tree again, and it was *the* last time he ever did!

Big Jim was truly the neighborhood "fix it" man. He had tools for everything and owned a bunch of motorcycles, and bought the first ever model of the new Honda car. He was a long-distance bicycle rider also. He worked at one of the steel plants, operating the big overhead crane, loading up trucks and trains with rolled pipe. Big Jim was a great guy to have next door. Unfortunately, he was diagnosed with leukemia and didn't last very long. It left his wife, Kathy, to raise Jimmy and his older sister, Dawn. It was a pretty gut-wrenching time on Lincoln Street.

Years later I was back in California and on the fire department. Jimmy had come out and wanted to move out west. He's an amazing tool and die machinist, and there was a lot of opportunity for him. He still lived with his mom, and he ended up having a running battle with the people that moved into the Bender's place. They had a pack of dogs, and their German Shepherd was pretty aggressive. Their aggression was because they made them all stay outside in all types of inclement weather and never gave them any attention. The dogs would come up to Kathy's summer garden and tear up everything, eating the vegetables and flowers. Jimmy had enough. He went down and told them that if those dogs came up to his yard again, he was going to shoot them.

On a sunny day, my mom and dad had our house and yard looking fantastic. They went out for lunch while the real estate agent brought a couple to look at our house for the second time. They figured an offer was going to be made. She showed the couple all around the inside of the house and, of course, told how close everyone on the street was with each other. As they walked out onto the front porch . . .

A pack of dogs came running into the yard.

"You son of a bitch dogs!"

BLAM! BLAM! BLAM!

There was Jimmy, shooting the neighbors dogs right next to our front lawn! The dogs yipped and limped home as quick as they could. The real estate agent was aghast. There goes the sale!

The couple just walked over to speak with Jimmy, came back and made an offer on the house. They still live there to this day.

Jimmy moved in with me in California for a while, and now owns a giant farm in Australia with his wife. He's really a long way from that gravel road!

Whenever I make it back to the hometown, I take a drive by for old times' sake and smile, thinking about all the great memories. When I spoke with Jim about adding his story to the book, he said it was OK, as long as I mentioned him running naked into our yard, chased by his dad, when he was little!

THE GHOST OF HENRY PUTT AND OTHER FIREHOUSE TALES

MY PARENTS

My mom was a lifelong smoker, which did neither her nor my dad any health favors. They celebrated their fiftieth wedding anniversary in June of 2000 with an Alaskan cruise, something my dad had wanted to do for years. I met them in Vancouver after they came back down the coast and celebrated with them for two days. We had a fun time exploring the city and eating at some very lovely restaurants. Who knew that it was such a good idea at the time?

When they arrived back home in Pennsylvania, my mom was telling her sister, my Aunt Pegge, all about their trip, when suddenly she slumped over and went into full cardiac arrest. She had a sudden, massive stroke. My dad, being the old war-horse firefighter and EMT, started CPR on her right away. She survived that event, but was in seriously bad shape. She was finally moved from the hospital to a nursing home facility, which she absolutely hated. She wanted out! Her incredible stubbornness shined through. A few weeks later, at the way too young age of seventy, she passed away.

My dad was gutted. They had been together through thick and thin, good and bad, and now had life easy. They had sold our house on Lincoln Street and moved into an apartment years earlier. No yard work and minimal cleaning: just lock the door and travel. They had a small trailer at a campground and would spend weeks there enjoying life every summer.

I flew back and gave the eulogy at her funeral. Telling the story to a packed funeral home full of friends and relatives of how she blew up the little trailer when I was young, and other heartwarming stories. It was hard for everyone to believe she had passed at such a young age.

I invited my dad to come out and stay with me in California; a month later he showed up at my doorstep.

We had a wonderful time going to a few Los Angeles Kings games, and I even got him to try some sushi! A huge feat for a guy that grew up on Midwest meat and potatoes. We went up for another helicopter ride and really enjoyed hanging out together.

Right before he was scheduled to fly home, I invited him to come ride along at the fire department with me. I was on the ladder truck at Station Eight; we had an open seat for him to ride in: it is a tiller truck with a firefighter steering the back. He loved coming to the station that day. Just being around the crew made him feel alive again. We ran a few of the usual false alarms and a couple minor traffic collisions. We whipped up a really nice dinner, and all the guys were happy to have him hang with us. He had met most of them on west coast visits in the past.

After dinner we were dispatched for a fire at an International House of Pancakes. There was a fire in the kitchen that was out of control. We rolled down with our barn mates, Engine Eight, as well as Engine Six and Engine Seven, to find a large plume of heavy smoke puffing out of the roof vents.

I was actually happy, as my dad would get to see us in action.

We took to the top with the power saws and started venting the flat roof. We were cutting big holes in it to let the smoke and heat out so the engine company could advance their attack hose lines. After we got it knocked down, I walked over to the parapet to look over and see where my dad was. He was standing next to the battalion chief, grinning ear to ear. The chief took him to the store to help get us some cold drinks. The long-time firefighter in him was coming out, and if we would have let him, he would have loved to don some gear, come up and cut some ventilation holes with us!

We got back to the firehouse after a few hours and he helped us clean up the equipment and reload hose. It was the most I had seen him smile since mom died. She passed in August and it was now October.

A few days later he told me he was going to move out to California. I was still single, so I had no problem getting a house with him. He, however, wanted his own place, and didn't want to intrude. I gave him a hug, thanked him for trying sushi after all these years, and told him we appreciated his help at the fire. He said he had loved watching us in action!

I was working Thanksgiving Day at Station Eight. We always played ball hockey in our self-titled Parking Lot Hockey League. The phone rang and it was my dad. I was out of breath and sweating like crazy as we spoke. He told me he had been calling all our relatives that day and it was great to speak with everyone. He let me know he found a place in California he was interested in and wanted to come back out for Christmas to check it out. A great plan!

We spoke for a few more minutes and I told him I would call him the following week.

He died in his sleep that Sunday night from complications from Congestive Heart Failure. I think it was a broken heart.

He was only 71.

This book is supposed to be all fun. But this was important to tell. Call the people you love. Spend time with them.

I have a mantra I follow: "Life is good, hug your friends."

Do it.

Fred Raymond and Mary Lou getting married in 1950

THE CHIEF'S OFFICES

Firefighters love to think they know everything that is going on in the department. They always want to know the "scoop," or think they have the newest, "hot scoop!" Throwing down some fake memos or phone messages on the chief's desk would always be the best way to reel them in, hook, line, and sinker.

In Pennsylvania, the chief had a small office and an attached private bathroom. We would get the key from the on-duty captain to clean it every Sunday morning. We didn't have a secretary dedicated to just the fire department, so he would have one of the secretaries upstairs in the mayor's office type all the memos. Old Dad would write them out by hand, as he wasn't too adept with a typewriter.

We had four different shifts, and most of the firefighters were happy with who they worked with. There were a couple of guys that really didn't get along too well with each other, and on a department of only twenty-nine firefighters, it's best to keep them apart and happy.

I've a knack for imitating handwriting and forging signatures, so I put that skill to good use. The Sunday after Thanksgiving I ended up working downtown to cover a vacation day. I put a memo on his desk that had an all new shift staffing. Of course, I put all the people that really didn't work well together on one shift for the downtown and East Side firehouses. As I was cleaning the chief's toilet, one of the notorious snoops came in to see what scoop he could find. When he saw the memo with all of the names on all new shifts, he hit the ceiling! He called the other crew members in to show them his find. Old Dad was moving everyone around effective January First.

They flipped!

As they ran into the kitchen to bitch about everything, I grabbed the memo off the desk and off I went, locking up the office.

The rumors flew around the department in about an hour. They couldn't ask the chief about it as that would give away their snooping in his office. I went back to the East Side and let the Night Commander know what I had done. The rumors went wild and I think it probably ruined a few Christmastimes with worry. A few of the captains hinted around with the chief to see if any changes were coming, but he just looked at them like they were crazy.

When January came and went and no one was moved, everyone was relieved.

In California at Station One, we would have to wash the fire chief's windows every Saturday and clean the carpeting every once in a while. I would often put a bogus memo or a phone message on the chief's desk before the rest of the crew came in to help. They ranged from rehiring firefighters that had left for other departments to shift changes and promotions.

It was like shooting the proverbial ducks in a barrel.

I did a highly scientific study with the Viking one shift. We wondered how long a rumor would take to be told at Station One and find its way to the farthest away firehouse, Station Six. We made up some bogus claim about drug testing being started every day for all the stations and just tossed it out at the morning coffee at shift change. I just mentioned it and the Viking said he had heard that also. That's all it took. By eight o'clock that evening, the captain from Station Six was calling, all shook up about the new drug testing rules.

Well, that didn't take very long!

I've been "gotten" a few times over the years with a few good ones as well.

Firehouse pranks are the best. There is only one rule: Don't mess with anyone's safety gear

The Craziest Call Chronicles

Firefighters around the world see some things happen every shift that if it was in a movie script, you would be hard pressed to believe it was real. Over the years I've seen some of the most unreal things happen, just when I thought I had "seen it all!"

Remember, when we're in training during the academy, we have no clue what we're about to encounter for the next twenty or thirty years.

One

It was a warm summer evening and a couple was sitting on their back porch enjoying a cold beverage. Their home was on the other side of the giant cement block sound wall along the freeway. They heard tires screeching and then a crash. Two seconds later a body came flying out of the sky and landed in their flower garden with a thud!

The flying man stood up and brushed himself off and then fell over back to the ground and started snoring. They couldn't believe it. The guy smelled like booze and had passed out. They called 911 and wondered how the hell he came out of the sky.

I was working on Truck One that evening; we responded with Engine Three and Engine Six. The truck and Engine Three were dispatched to the traffic collision reported on the freeway and Engine Six responded to treat the superhuman flying patient in the garden.

When we arrived on scene, there was a trapped man in an old Ford F150 pickup truck, with the windshield completely gone. The paramedics declared him dead, as the steering wheel had really crushed his chest in. Engine Six was on the other side of the thirty-five-foot block wall tending to the passenger. He didn't seem to have a scratch on him, but was drunk off his ass.

These two numbskulls had been at a bar and powered down way too many drinks. Witnesses said they were going over a hundred miles per hour, swerving through all four lanes, when they went too far over to the shoulder and caught the dirt. They spun out and flew down the embankment and came to a very sudden halt at the drainage ditch. The steering wheel kept the driver in; however, the passenger was ejected and flew completely over the wall, landing in the backyard of the home at the end of the cul-de-sac!

The witnesses assured us they saw two men flying through the air!

We radioed Engine Six and they confirmed only one patient. We walked down toward the wall in the high weeds with some high-powered flashlights and made the discovery. There was a second passenger that was in the truck, and his pole-vaulting skills weren't so good. He hit the wall about three feet from clearing it, leaving part of his scalp on the block wall, crumpling down to earth in a bloody mess.

And yes, one of the smart asses I was working with asked if I had the Magic Blanket with me, because that guy really needed it.

Superman lived, with only cuts from flying through the windshield and a few bruises from the garden landing. The police forensics officer estimated he went forty-two feet up out of the truck, thirty feet across the wall and into the yard, and thirty-nine feet down to the petunias!

Two

Pagers and cell phone stores were opening up all across the city. They were the newest hot items to own and business was brisk. A store opened just around the corner from Station Three and we would stop in there once in a while to say hi to the owner and check out the new line of electronics. He had a great selection of merchandise and was becoming the busiest store in the city.

We got the call in the late afternoon: "Engine Three, Engine One with police responding, shooting with multiple victims at the electronics store, 1242 Grove Street, one of the injured is a suspect, proceed with caution."

We arrived at the same time the first police officer came skidding in. We waited outside as he went in with his gun drawn. He gave the OK for us to come in and start working on the two patients. Engine One was coming from way across town so we knew we were on our own for a few minutes. The owner was telling us as fast as he could what had happened. He was still really amped up from the Wild West shootout he had just been involved in!

A man and woman had entered the store with guns drawn and yelling for him to empty the cash register and to put some pagers and phones into a bag. He had a revolver under the cash register and acted like he was getting the cash out of the drawer, but came up firing! The woman pulled the trigger on her handgun, but didn't have a bullet in the chamber. He got the drop on her easily. However, he took a hail of bullets from her partner. The owner had two bullet holes through his hand and a couple to the chest and arms. He managed to shoot both of them, getting the man in the chest. The robber staggered out the door, leaving his wounded female accomplice behind, and made it to a local emergency room two cities away, to awaiting police officers with guns drawn and handcuffs ready.

The female was lying on her back unconscious and that's when we noticed something none of us had ever seen before. Blood bubbles were steadily blowing out of her bicep area, like a tire leak of air.

What the hell?

She had no other wounds we could find. The owner had shot her in the arm that she was pointing her gun with, and the bullet struck her humerus bone, that goes between the shoulder and elbow. It ricocheted right up the bone and into her lung. She was slowly dying of a pneumothorax. Hop and I worked up the owner; Bailey and the Bhagwan worked her up. Engine One arrived and pitched in with everything they had to keep both patients alive. The owner's chest wounds were amazingly not serious, as the bullets lodged in muscle and didn't make it to his heart or lungs, but the holes in his hands were pretty bad. You could look right through them.

As he came up shooting with his right hand, he shielded himself with his other hand. It must have slowed the two bullets down enough to not penetrate deep into his body. It was "superhero like" that he blocked the bullets.

The robbers lived and were convicted of this and some previous crimes they were wanted for. The pager store opened three weeks later after window and wall bullet-hole repairs, reloading, and hand surgery.

Three

The city had a pretty big gang problem in the late eighties and early nineties. The police department was trying to stay on it, but the gangs were really well organized and it seemed like something was happening every night in town that was their handiwork. We had home grown gangs doing business all across the city and the heavy hitters from the Los Angeles area were moving into the suburban drug trade. It seemed that for a while we were running on a shooting victim every week.

I was working my usual shift at Station Three with Joey, the Bhagwan, and Hop. It was an unusually quiet day and we were getting some needed firehouse maintenance items handled.

"Engine Three, Engine Two, multiple shooting victims at the corner of Campus and Pine, use caution, PD has a delay due to call volume."

We approached the scene cautiously, but Joey figured the shooters weren't sticking around to sign any autographs. About a half a block away we could see the carnage. There was blood flowing onto the street; the front seat passenger was lying half in the vehicle with his legs in the car, half on his back on the blood-drenched pavement. The back-seat passenger was slumped against the door, bleeding profusely.

We stopped the rig about thirty feet away and took a good look around before we got out to get the medic gear. A bystander ran up and said the shooters had left in two separate cars. We jumped off the rig and got to work. I remember telling Joey that I hope these guys were all dead, because working them up was going to be one hell of a mess!

As we got to the car, the victims were all still breathing. One in the front seat and two in the back seat. All of them had more bullet holes in them than I had ever seen before. Joey radioed for two more medic engine companies and two additional ambulances. We each took a patient and started doing what we could to stop the flow of blood on each patient.

I took the gang member in the front seat. He had bullet entry wounds in his legs and arms, and had taken one right into his left eyeball! Now, if that was a normal person, they would be dead, that would be the end of it, but we always said that you just can't kill a gangbanger, and these guys were living proof.

I put some four-by-four bandages on his eye socket and wrapped some gauze around his head to hold it in place. I wrapped as many wounds as I could on his extremities, slipping and sliding in all of the blood on the street. We got IV fluids into the three of them and started to get them packaged up for the ambulance ride. The other incoming units started arriving to give us some much-needed help.

The driver, who bailed out and hid under the car when the shooting started, and various witnesses started telling the police the story. A rival group of gang members pulled up in two cars and cut them off. They got out with guns in each hand, blazing away like a scene out of the movie *Reservoir Dogs*.

My patient started crashing hard. The Sheriff Department's helicopter was overhead. They're outfitted for medical transport and asked if we needed assistance. Joey had them land at Station Three, as there's a huge grass area behind the station and training center tower.

We managed to get all three of them to the hospital still breathing. The clean up after this call was one of the biggest messes of all time. Blood was all over everything, including our uniforms, the medical gear, and the rig. We were out of service for about two hours getting everything sanitized and put back together.

We wondered if they lived or died, but didn't find any information about them, as they went to three different trauma centers. For years I wondered about that kid that was shot in the eye.

Years later, in 2010, I was about three weeks from retiring. I was working a shift trade at my old stomping grounds, Station Three. We ran on a call for a seizure. The crew was telling me on the way that this guy was a "frequent flyer," a person that has the department out often for their ailments. They told me he had been shot in a gun battle and was now having some serious issues from it. I thought, "Could it be? Nope, that dude had to have died."

When we walked into the house, the patient was sitting in a chair covered in sweat. He had a massive seizure and was slowly coming around out of his postictal stage. His mom was there clutching her Rosary beads, crying and praying in Spanish. I took a look at his left eye. He had a huge scar above and below it and you could tell it was glass.

Hmmm . . . I had to ask.

"Hey amigo, were you shot in a gun battle with three of your friends about twenty years ago?"

He looked at me really puzzled, like how in the world does this guy know that info.

"And you were flown to the hospital in a helicopter that day, right?"

"Si, that was me and my homies."

"I was there on that call and helped take care of you that day. You all should have died that afternoon."

He couldn't believe it and got up and hugged me, and then told his mom that I helped save him. She came over and started hugging and kissing me on the cheek and blessing me with her Rosary beads, all in Spanish.

He told me that they had moved away from town when he was released from the hospital, and he has been out of the gang business ever since. He had had fifteen gunshot wounds and was in the hospital for over a month. They moved back to town recently to help some older relatives.

He hugged me again tightly and thanked me. The firefighters at Station Three had heard about that call but didn't put it together that this could be one of the survivors all this time later.

He told me that the other two victims also survived, but with serious issues. I couldn't believe it.

It took two decades, but I'm glad I found out how he made out, because I would have still wondered about that call all these years later!

Four

The city, unfortunately, had a homeless issue, like many other towns across America. We would often get called out on the same people over and over again and many would camp out at the various parks across town. Our city did as much as they could over the years to help feed and house as many people as possible.

One evening I was working on Engine Two. We received a call for a possible dumpster fire in an industrial area. When we arrived, there was no fire, just four empty soup cans on each corner of the cement block wall around the dumpster slightly smoldering with burning paper in them. There was a man standing there with a motorcycle helmet on.

I was puzzled. "Hey buddy, what's going on here tonight?"

"High acceleration to get off of being earthbound and into the galaxy, I have it all figured out, I just need a few more minutes to charge the ship."

"Um, OK, what's the ship you're using, this dumpster?"

"Yes, I have been working on it all day, it's almost charged and I'll be getting in soon. Wanna come along?"

"No thanks, sounds fun though, but I don't want to throw off your calculations and weight and balance."

"Good point, but if you have a pencil, I could do it quickly."

The captain radioed for a police unit. This poor fellow was delusional and we didn't want him to get hurt.

"Sir, what are the cans doing sitting on the four corners?"

"Those are my charging pods, they will put enough energy into the ship to propel me to outer space."

"Oh man, that's so cool, how did you come up with this idea?"

"I have been planning it all week and when I found this ship, I knew it would work."

He lifted the lid of the dumpster to show us some donuts and an apple and banana he was going to go into outer space with.

I had to ask. "Do you think that's enough food for the trip and do you need some Tang?"

"The trip will only be a day or two, I'll be fine."

"Toilet paper?"

"I have some napkins here for that, but hopefully I won't have to poop as it is weightlessness up there."

We had run on hundreds of homeless people with all sorts of serious issues in the past, but this gentleman was by far the best. I couldn't help wondering if he was a scientist that had mental or addiction issues or if he just liked rockets and outer space. A lot of the people we dealt with were belligerent, drugged-up, or drunk. This man was really likeable and polite as could be.

"OK, guys, can you stand by for my blast off in case it catches on fire?"

"Sure, we'll watch you and make sure it's safe."

He opened the dumpster lid and climbed in. It had been emptied that day, so the only thing in it was his food and napkins. He lowered the lid and started his countdown.

"Three. Two. One. IGNITION!" he shouted.

He made all sorts of rocket sound effects and started talking to "mission control." The police arrived and we asked the officers to give it a few minutes. We really didn't want to wreck this guy's fantasy flight.

After a few minutes I asked him how the flight was going, and if he needed some hot coffee.

The big plastic dumpster lid slowly opened; he was grinning ear to ear. "That was awesome! Can we go for coffee now?"

"Sure buddy, that was a great lift off!"

The officers took him for evaluation to the hospital, making sure he would get a warm cup of coffee to go with his donuts. We never saw him again and I still wonder what happened to him, the coolest homeless astronaut of all time.

Five

Engine Four was called to an apartment for a report of a 911 call with a hang up. They responded with the police department, as these calls can range from little kids calling by mistake or people seriously injured.

When they arrived at the apartment, they were met by a maintenance worker that said he heard a yell for help and then nothing. The door was locked, so they forced it open to quite the scene.

The living room's all glass top coffee table was broken, and there were bloody tracks leading down the hallway. They followed them into the bathroom where they found the source.

A middle-aged man was dead on the floor in a giant pool of blood. He didn't have any pants on, and there was what appeared to be a pool cue stick . . . stuck in his ass. (Yes, you read that right.)

The crew couldn't figure this one out and thought it might be a murder scene. They went back to the living room, where the TV was on but just showing some fuzz and snow, like a VHS tape had stopped. The empty VHS box next to the recorder was a porno movie.

Hmmm . . .

On the couch by the table was some hand lotion and K-Y Jelly. The pieces were coming together.

The man had been watching porn in the living room, with his hands on the glass coffee table and a pool cue up his butt. Yes, you just read that correctly. He must have been choking his chicken pretty seriously when the table shattered under his weight, cutting his wrist and jamming the pool cue into his insides, causing massive internal bleeding. He crawled to the bathroom, with the phone in his hand and must have gotten a call to the dispatch center before losing consciousness.

I'm really glad we weren't the ones that had to explain this to his wife when she came home from work.

I'm not sure even the Magic Blanket was saving this pervert.

Ouch!

SEPTEMBER 11, 2001

As an odd coincidence, I'm sitting at my desk writing the story of September 11 exactly nineteen years later to the day. I've been watching some of the news reports about the services at "Ground Zero" and reading many tributes on social media. It still seems so surreal to me.

I was base jumping often and Steve had called me to ask about going on the Angel Falls trip. I had six days off coming up and decided to drive up to the Perrine Bridge in Twin Falls, Idaho, to do some legal bridge jumps and work on my exits. The thought of going to Venezuela had me excited and worried a bit. I wanted to be as prepared as I possibly could.

I left my firehouse packed up for six days of travel on September 5. I made it to Idaho and did fifteen jumps in three days from the 486-foot-high span over the Snake River. It's a great spot to practice exits and is only a two-second delay after leaving the bridge before you need to deploy the parachute.

I decided to make a run down to Auburn, California, and visit my friends, Marty and Karla, on the way back home. Marty taught me how to base jump, and there's a giant bridge nearby their house that we often jumped together. Marty and I did a few bridge jumps in the middle of the night and had a great time as usual. The county fairgrounds in town—where we had done some Fourth of July exhibition jumps into over the years—was hosting a demolition derby. Nothing says "Americana" like a small-town event like this with some cotton candy and snow cones while watching old cars smash into each other! We had a fantastic time for two days, and I decided to head on home by way of Yosemite National Park to make a leap off of El Capitan.

Making a jump in Yosemite is illegal. If you get caught, they charge you with some ridiculous law from the 1920s:"aerial delivery without a permit." El Cap is just over 3,000 feet tall and is a fantastic big wall base jump. You can take about a ten-second delay down the face of it before opening. Like any big cliff jump, you need to track away from the granite. It's not wise to jump it alone in case of a landing injury, but I was feeling like I really needed a leap off it before getting back to the firehouse on the eleventh. This was going to be my third leap off that giant hunk of granite. I did the first jump with Mark, and had just jumped El Cap a few months previously with Steve, before he headed back to England.

It was a gorgeous day in the park on that September 10. Half Dome and El Cap were shining brightly that afternoon as they stood tall watching over the valley floor. My plan was to leave my truck at a campground, hike up the trail beside Yosemite Falls, and work my way out to the exit point on top. I packed my base rig in a backpack, filled a few water bottles, and tossed in a bag of my "Uncle Bob" rations, Tootsie Rolls, and trail mix, and headed off for the couple of hour trek to the top. Uncle Bob would have loved this adventure, and he would have made a great getaway driver.

Part way up the trail is an area called Columbia Rock. I was in no hurry, as I had hours to make it to the exit point before sunset, my planned launch window. There were two people having lunch there: a dad and his daughter from London, about sixtyish and thirtyish in age. I sat down and said hello. We started talking about the view and how amazing the weather was this fine day. They told me that the mom and the son hated to fly and never, ever left London. They, however, would go somewhere on a father, daughter vacation every year. They told me about all of the places they had been to together over the years, ever since the daughter was five years old.

We had an enjoyable conversation that afternoon, laughing about how Brits and Americans were so much alike yet so incredibly different. They asked where I was going to hike to. I let them in on my secret and asked if they wanted to stick around at the road that runs along the bottom of El Capitan to watch me jump. They were "gobsmacked," to use their exact words, at what I was going to do! They really wanted to stay but had to get back to San Francisco for an early morning flight back to Heathrow. We talked for another hour, before they decided it was time they needed to head out. One thing they both mentioned to me was that they thought security at US airports was rather lax. At the time, I didn't realize how profound that observation would become in the morning.

They wished me luck and both of them hugged me goodbye.

My plan was to hike up before it got too dark and make the leap. I always figured a bear would get me up there before a jumping accident ever did. I looked out at the tree line as I started up along the falls. It was starting to get windy. I made it to the top of the falls and didn't like what I was seeing. The trees were now really swaying back and forth and it was getting worse. I had a decision to make. Go to the exit point and hope it calms down, or head back down now and call it a day. The thought of hiking down in the dark really scared me. You know, those damn bears, and mountain lions! But it's not wise to jump when the conditions suck. I had a few friends over the years that pushed the limits with the weather and it didn't go well for them.

I sat at the top of the falls and enjoyed the view for about another hour or so, munching on the last of my trail mix. I started laughing, thinking about how scared I was on my first jump here with Mark a few years earlier. I was wishing he was with me on this one. El Cap has been around a few million years and wasn't going anywhere, so I figured I'll just head back down in the daylight and get back to Southern California, as I had to be on duty at Station Eight at 7 a.m. I made my way back down and headed on the road, smiling about what a fantastic six days I had enjoyed while I mauled a few In-N-Out burgers on the highway south.

I made it to my firehouse about 1 a.m. and crashed out quietly and quickly in one of the TV room recliners because I didn't want to wake up the eight firefighters on duty. I fell in to a really deep sleep.

"Reaper, wake up, we're under attack!"

My pal Dan was yelling at me to wake up. It was almost shift change and the crew had the morning news on. Airliners were flying into buildings in New York City and the Pentagon.

I crowded into the small TV room next to the station's dining room with everyone. We couldn't believe our eyes. And then . . .

"Engine Eight, Truck Eight, Engine Six, Engine Five, Alert 33 at the airport, United Airlines making an emergency landing, unknown problem!"

As I climbed up into the tiller box of the ladder truck, I wondered for a second if we should get our bullet proof vests out and put them on? What the hell was going to happen? Were we going to be met by terrorists with machine guns? Was the airliner going to crash land, or even make it to the airport?

When we arrived at the airport the airliner was just touching down. A warning light in the cockpit had come on and the pilots had been told the news about the attacks over the radio by air traffic control. They were told to land at the nearest airport immediately. Luckily, there were no terrorists on board and it was just a faulty sensor on one of the engines.

We really didn't know what to expect the rest of that day. It was the Party Bob's first day as a battalion chief. I saw him at the airport and we both had pretty worried looks on our faces. His wife is a flight attendant for American Airlines, and I was worried. Luckily, she wasn't flying this day. We drove back to the firehouse, wondering what was going on.

When we watched the towers collapse, I could only wonder how many firefighters from the FDNY hockey teams that I knew were there. I also knew a lot of New York skydivers that worked in Manhattan. Like everyone in America, I was sick to my stomach that day and couldn't fathom what and how this had happened.

I think I can speak for thousands of brother and sister firefighters around the world that were watching from afar that day: it's probably the most helpless feeling we ever had watching a disaster unfold around the world.

I thought back to my dad, and how I hounded him about us going to New York City for mutual aid when I was a little kid. And I couldn't stop thinking about the father and daughter that were flying back home to London that morning. I really hope they made it off the ground in San Francisco and back to the UK without any issues.

I had many friends respond with their fire department's search and rescue teams, from around the nation, that dug on the "pile" for weeks searching for bodies. Many of the FDNY firefighters I know were there for months and some of them are now retired due to the long-term health effects they suffered.

The Ray Pfieffer Foundation helps out everyone that's still suffering health effects from that fateful day, and it's my honor and privilege to donate the proceeds of this book to the foundation.

Nineteen years later, and I will never forget . . .

JUST PICKING UP OUR PAYCHECKS, SIR!

Flying a helicopter around Southern California is really the only way to travel! There's nothing quite like zipping over the 91 freeway at rush hour, looking down at a million cars inching along. I would often take friends up for flights around the area as I was building my hours toward a commercial rating.

One day I was at the gym with the Party Bob. It was a payday Friday, way back before auto deposit was a thing. We were on days off and the thought of a Friday drive out and back to get paid seemed like a daunting task on such a lovely afternoon.

"Hey Bob, let's fly out to pick up our checks. I'll do it if you buy sushi tonight."

"*In*, Reaper!"

I phoned the airport and asked the flight school to get a helicopter fueled and ready for us.

It was a fantastic day for flying. Our fire chief, Big Fred, had given me the permission to land at our training center any time I would like to fly in. There's a large grass area behind the drill tower and our Station Three that's perfect for a helicopter landing zone. We lifted off from Long Beach Airport and headed over the giant parking lots known as the freeways. Cars were barely moving in either direction. Yes, we made fun of those poor bastards as we cruised along at ninety miles per hour. We turned a two-hour drive into a twenty-minute flight.

The training center was often used for various classes. There is a five-story drill tower and a big classroom that other departments often utilized and where state classes could also be held. On this day, as we circled to check the landing area, a large group of firefighters from various agencies were out on the grass lawn. There was a state-run Hazardous Materials course going on and everyone was on a break.

I circled for a few minutes and no on caught on that we needed the lawn cleared so we could touch down. I started descending and slowed our speed, which makes the blade flap noise a little louder. Everyone looked up with a perplexed look on their faces as I started a steep approach. Everyone cleared the grass area and watched as we slowly came in for a nice landing. I let the engine idle for a few minutes for the cool down and then shut the engine down.

A bunch of the students came up, bewildered as to who we were and what we were doing.

"That was cool, who are you guys?"

We introduced ourselves to the group that had gathered to check out the helicopter.

"What are you doing flying in, one of them asked?"

Bob and I just smiled.

"We're here to pick up our paychecks, of course, it's Friday."

"You guys at this department make way too much money!"

And that was it. The story went out to twenty or thirty different fire departments that firefighters on our department fly helicopters to get paid!

Taking Alec for his first helicopter flight

I would often take Horrible up flying with me. Joey and Hop had set up helispots for me to land at their large rural homes. We would often fly out and visit on summer days, swimming and having lunch with them. When Hop moved into his new house, he mowed a nice helipad for me; I flew out and gave everyone rides for his house warming party.

Getting a helicopter rating sure made life in Southern California a little easier and a lot more fun!

The Wedding Rehearsal

Jethro Bodine finally proposed to his lovely girlfriend, Anne. The wedding was going to be quite the fantastic production. They were getting married at one of the biggest churches in the city, and then they were going to be driven on the ladder truck to get some great photos at a local park. A couple of us from the department were honored to be in the wedding party. The week before the big day, they hosted a rehearsal at the church. It went smooth and all of us were pretty excited for the event of the year.

I lived pretty far away at the beach and decided to stay at their house after the reception, as I had to be on duty the next morning. We got back to their house after dinner and decided to celebrate on the back porch with a couple of cold Coronas. Their house was just a few blocks away from Station One, so we would hear the units head out on calls often, as the station was very busy.

"Guys, guys!" Anne was screaming at us from their living room. "The house across the street is on fire!"

We jumped up and raced to the front door, just as Engine One and Truck One were arriving. The two-story house across the street had fire blowing out of the upstairs windows!

Joey was working as the captain on Engine One. That caught us be surprise as he was my regular captain on Engine Three. He had been called in to cover a sick day. Joey radioed to Engine Four to lay a supply line. Bodine and I were in shorts and flip flops, but were ready to help. We told Joey we would hand jack a four-inch supply line the half a block to the hydrant. I ran it to the plug and Bodine clamped the hose and called for water.

The house was really burning like hell now. Engine Four was just arriving. The homes on either side were starting to catch fire. The truck company was inside looking for trapped victims.

We stretched a handline to each side of the house and started cooling down the exposures. The other units arrived and picked up what we started. Bodine and I made sure the pump operator had what he needed for water flow.

The battalion chief arrived, and had a puzzled look on his face when he saw us.

"What the hell are you two doing here, out of safety gear?" He inquired.

"Chief, I live across the street and we saw what was happening."

I figured that was it. The department had been cracking down on everything lately, and all the ranks were getting reprimanded left and right for silly little things. I just knew we would be getting called into a chief's office over this one.

The fire was knocked down quickly after the additional units arrived, so we headed back to the house. Joey yelled at us.

"Thanks, you guys, that was smart thinking and helped a lot."

We went back for another beer on the porch, laughing about how random it was to have the neighbor's house catch on fire the night of his rehearsal dinner. Luckily, they weren't home, as they were an elderly couple that would have had trouble getting out, most likely.

"Maybe the universe is trying to tell you something, Bodine."

A few days later a letter marked "Confidential" arrived at the station in the department mail. I figured this was it, my invitation to the chief's office for an ass chewing.

Nope!

It was an "Attaboy" memo from El Jefe! I couldn't believe it. Joey had discussed our actions with the battalion chief, and they agreed that we helped the house fire from getting out of control, and we acted, with disregard to our own safety, to save property.

Classic. I called Bodine, he had also received a letter, and he couldn't believe it either!

That Saturday, *the* wedding of the year was fabulous. The photos on the ladder truck turned out amazing. They had the iconic hamburger company In-N-Out cater the reception. It was one of the most fun wedding receptions of all time.

BODINE'S BIRTHDAY

J ethro Bodine was turning thirty, and the bash was going to be pretty epic. Anne hosted a party at their house, with all sorts of food, a keg of beer, and lots of other drinks.

There were firefighters from the department and surrounding areas in attendance. Some of his high school pals were there also. It was a warm evening and the stars were out, sparkling brightly, on a cloudless night. Anne had set up a couple folding tables for assorted food platters and for the giant birthday cake with a huge icing fire truck on top . The music was blaring and the party was in full swing!

Bodine had the idea of taking the keg of beer up onto the roof to have some drinks and better see the stars. About ten of us went up and perched on the peak. We gave Bodine's best friend since they were little, Ronnie, one job. Keep a hand on the keg. Ronnie had just been hired with us.

Someone told a hilarious story, and Ronnie cracked up, letting go of the keg. It teetered one way, and then the other! When he lunged to get ahold of it again, it tilted right toward the back yard, and started it's roll down the roof.

"LOOK OUT!" we all yelled at once to the handful of people surrounding the food tables. They all scattered as the keg, almost in slow motion, went airborne off of the rain gutter and headed straight for the table with the giant cake on it.

Wham!

Like some sort of cartoon, the keg hit the end of the table with great force, flipping it up in the air, like a seesaw, and launched the yet to be cut cake, cheese platters, and assorted other food across the yard, splattering a few guests!

"Ronnie, we gave you *one* job, you dumbass!"

What a thirtieth to remember.

Ronnie just filed out his retirement papers. Where does time go?

WHAT A CAREER

I often wonder what my life would have been like had I never become involved in the fire service. I think about a life of pouring hot steel like my grandfather or selling life insurance or being an accountant. I could have never had an office job, that's for sure, and I wouldn't have met so many amazing human beings that greatly influenced my life. And I sure as hell wouldn't have any good stories for a book!

Some of you may have been wondering if I ever made it out of the firefighter ranks. When I first got on the job, my goal was to work my way up to be the chief of department. I'm sure a lot of us have big lofty goals after we make it through probation. Somewhere along the line, I started making money skydiving and flying helicopters on my days off. I never took the firefighting job for the money, and I always liked being at the forefront of the action, be it cutting people out of crashed vehicles or venting a roof or searching a building for victims. Driving a desk never seemed like much fun to me.

The other thing I loved about staying in the firefighter ranks was the ability to trade shifts with so many different people, ensuring a lot of time off in a row, allowing me to travel the world. When we started shelving the old ladder trucks with the baskets and getting all tiller trucks, that finally sealed the deal for me. I spent the last decade of my career steering the opposite way behind Jethro Bodine. I also worked with two fantastic captains those last ten or so years. Jim and then Kurt. Those two made coming to work a lot of fun, and they really knew what they were doing on calls because both had been on the job for years and were fantastic captains.

The thought of messing that up kept me a firefighter until I retired.

When I now think back on all of the amazing people I worked with, I can only hope that I had an effect on some of the rookies I worked with as these people had on me through the years. Some of you might wonder why there are no female firefighters written about. On my two different career departments, there was only one female firefighter that I worked with. She resigned to go to nursing school after I was on the job in California for only a year. She really was a ground breaker to get hired in 1980. She left the department after about five years on the job. We never had many women apply back then, and now it's not uncommon to see women on fire apparatus all across the nation. The fire service has been moving in the right direction for the last couple of decades.

From Q Ball teaching a bunch of high school kids how to put out fires to Old Dad sticking his neck out by giving a young Ohioan a chance and a great job to Red, Steve, and others who taught me the ropes when I was a snot-nosed nineteen-year-old, many older firefighters had me well prepared for emergencies and also showed me the fun side of the job. Chief Pish always told me how important it was to stay in good physical shape for my entire career, and Wild Bill had the patience of a saint. Both were loyal to the folks that worked under their guidance in fire prevention.

Chief Doan taught me how to stay calm in the face of adversity at an emergency. He was calm, cool, and collected. I had the honor of working with him on his very last shift before he retired. We laughed about all the calls we had been on together while drinking coffee until almost one in the morning and chasing the past in our memories.

When I was in fire prevention, we had a fire in a large hydrogen storage facility in town. Chief Doan was the incident commander and he asked me to go to the control room to keep him updated. There had been an explosion in the plumbing. We managed to get the fire out before it hit the gigantic storage sphere. If that blew up, half of the city would be leveled. I told him how scared shitless I was in that control room, radioing to him what the company's engineers were doing to off load the hydrogen. He said he knew how afraid I was, as it was evident in my voice. He then told me he was even more afraid. If it blew up it would have killed all of us. I couldn't believe he was scared. There wasn't a crack in his voice over the radio for the hours we were there!

Working with Joey at Station Three was an insight into one of the best fire captains and first paramedics we ever had on the department. I've also had some of the best firefighter partners on the job anywhere. I saved Hop in a house fire one afternoon and he saved me on a brush fire on the side of the freeway. Those stories will have to come out in the next book.

I tried to take what I learned from everyone and apply it over the years. There were a few officers on the department, just like anywhere and in any job, that were in a few pay grades over their heads. I tried to avoid those folks; however, sometimes it's inevitable that paths will cross over the years.

Writing this book has been a lot of fun and good therapy for me. I had to phone a lot of longtime friends to fill in some details about some of the stories. We would get laughing about stuff that happened over the years and a few people reminded me about a couple stories I had forgotten about.

I knew I was getting ready to retire and my time with the department was coming to an end. A few months before I put in for retirement, we got a call for an apartment complex on fire at two in the morning. I was working on the truck company with Kurt, Bodine, and a brand-new rookie.

The rookie, Justin, was so excited to be responding to this when he heard on the radio the arriving units giving the size-up of heavy smoke and fire coming out of a fourth-floor apartment. I could see the glow in the sky from the tiller box and just laughed. There was a time when I would be so upset if I missed out on a call like this. And all I could think of now was how hard we were going to work and how much my back and shoulders would be hurting!

I told Kurt and Bodine we were going to "Sunrise Service" tonight, and they agreed. We would be watching the sun come up on this call.

When we arrived, we laddered the building and started rooftop ventilation. We spent hours pulling roofing material off and getting to the hot spots. There comes a time when you know it's not your department any longer, and it's time to let the younger generation take over. When I was nineteen years old and the older guys in Pennsylvania would tell me that being a firefighter was a young person's job, I didn't understand what the hell they were talking about. But now, at almost 50, and after over three decades on the job, prying up tar paper forty feet up on a burned roof, I felt it was time to hang up the ax.

Alec was our best man at our wedding in Belize

Morgan's first firehouse visit a few years before I retired

I was single until I was forty-five years old. After I married Kristine, we had a daughter. She was four years old when we went to the pension office to fill out my retirement papers. She had on a Cinderella dress and her favorite princess shoes when we went to the office to sort everything and to officially retire. The clerk asked me how old my granddaughter was. We smiled and told her she was our daughter. The clerk was pretty embarrassed, but we just laughed and told her we couldn't believe we had a little one also! She said in her twenty years at the office, no one had retired with a four-year-old in tow before. We had a good laugh and I knew it was the right decision to get out at age fifty after thirty years.

We were in the opening stages of our new skydiving center and I was looking forward to a new chapter in my life. It was truly a family business, as my wife and niece ran the office, our son fueled the plane, and our daughter sold cookies to the skydivers.

At Fire Prevention Week Open House ready to watch dad
cut up a car for the crowd

Alec helping Morgan get ready for action

We operated our skydiving center in Oceanside, California, for four years, building it up from scratch into a thriving operation, then sold it to a long-time skydiving acquaintance from Europe. This allowed me time to concentrate on my once per year skydiving events in many different countries. We hosted one in Costa Rica, and fell in love with the area. We ended up buying a beach house and moved here permanently, selling everything we owned except my car and hockey gear. It's a much slower lifestyle here at the beach, and there's no snow to shovel. Living here with Kristine and Morgan is an adventure. Our son, Alec, lives in Southern California. He enjoys the city life.

With the kids on our first day at the new skydiving center

I still run a skydiving boogie somewhere around the globe each February. We've been to Belize, Palau, Nicaragua, and the Maldives. And of course, we jumped a few years in a row here in Costa Rica. I do a little consulting work with skydivers trying to open skydiving centers and help with a small operation here. It keeps me pretty busy, and I stay in touch with so many friends across the globe.

At my skydiving boogies, I have amazing jumpers from around the world help out. The following two photos are taken by Hall of Fame camera flyers, Bruno Brokken and Tom Sanders. Bruno has taken amazing pictures in free fall around the globe, including jumps at the North Pole. Tom filmed the skydiving scenes in the original Point Break movie and has been involved with James Bond and other movie and television productions for many years. Their artistry makes us all look good! And, we usually manage to make the covers of the world-wide skydiving magazines after an event.

Flying with friends over Tambor Bay, Costa Rica,
filmed by Bruno Brokken

Tom Sanders filmed us jumping over Kooddoo Island in the Maldives
with our pal, Joe, for his one thousandth skydive

February 2005, the very first jump into the Belize Great Blue Hole. A water landing followed by a SCUBA dive to 140 feet! At one o'clock, clockwise. Andy, Doak, Pacheco, Derek, me, Steve (from Angel Falls), Fred, and Janet. Photo by Andy Farrington

Doing a breakfast jump into downtown Kalispell, Montana, years ago with Doak, Teresa, Petey, and my partner in the bar and restaurant, Littleman. Of course we have parachutes on; Littleman is flying!

451

Before I started writing this book, I made a private Facebook page and invited about 200 friends to read some rough drafts of these stories. They were from different areas of my life. Skydivers, firefighters, relatives, and other friends read the stories and gave their input. Their encouragement and the time available now during a global pandemic, helped get me to finally commit to this ten year long dream of publishing a real book of my tales. Luckily, my cousin Jeremy has a publishing company and that made this process even easier for me.

While writing these stories I would often have to stop and reflect on the impact so many people have had on my life, smiling at how lucky I was to know such great human beings who dedicated so much of their lives to being there for friends, loved ones, and total strangers in their time of need.

The best way to end this life story of mine is to write an epilogue about all the characters in the tales.

EPILOGUE: THE CHARACTERS

Q Ball, the chief of the Ohio volunteer fire department, retired after about a decade of service with the department as the first ever paid firefighter. He lived to the ripe old age of eighty-eight, passing away due to natural causes. My older self wishes I had the chance to thank him for guiding a bunch of teenagers and showing us "the ropes" with such patience.

Old Dad, the Pennsylvania fire chief that hired me for my first full time firefighter position in 1979, retired a few years after I moved to California. Tragically, he died in his sixties. He was one of the hardest working people I've ever met. He still worked his side job for years after he became the fire chief.

His father was on the department and now his son, my old friend PT, carries on his legacy as a captain. I think a member of their family has been on the department there for almost one hundred years. I owe everything to Old Dad, as he hired a nineteen-year-old out-of-towner for a city job, and I'm sure he took some heat for it from some of the old school city council members, politics being politics in that city. My time spent there readied me for my career move to California.

Red, Luke, and Mad Dog are still living in the area. I try to catch up with them when I get back to visit. Red became the fire chief when Old Dad retired. He quit the department, retiring in protest, when the city closed the East Side firehouse a few years after I moved to California. He knew it was to the detriment of the safety of the citizens. His son, Kevin, is a captain there now, and lays carpet on his days off with Luke. Luke was elected to city council and eventually became the mayor. Mad Dog also served on city council. When we get together, the laughing and the stories get louder and funnier every year! I love those guys!

Steve, the Night Commander, is far more than a friend to me. We talk all the time (I actually just hung up from Whatsapping with him two minutes ago!). When we get together, we usually go somewhere for lunch and end up laughing so hard that we clear out the place! Steve is a giant man and loves to laugh; he's getting louder the more his hearing goes!

I couldn't have asked for a better friend after all these years. Working with him at the East Side firehouse was still, after all of these decades, the best job I've ever had. He now spends his time, in his early seventies, riding his bicycle and enjoying his grandkids. I spent lots of time at his house when I worked with him in the early '80s and have loved watching his kids grow up—and now they have kids of their own. I'm not gonna lie, *that* makes me feel a bit old! If someone asked for a role model to emulate, I would pick Steve. He's an amazing friend and family man. If you look in the dictionary under "Real Man," his photo should be there.

In Las Vegas with Steve on the left and Mooney, who just turned
ninety, the oldest living retiree from my PA department. We made the
Night Commander buy breakfast.

Howard, the Flying Frenchman, my longtime pal, is still
working his farm with his brother. He used to come out to visit
us in California for the winters. We always get together when
I visit the old hometown and have a fun time with some of our
old hockey buddies. His knees are giving him fits, so he doesn't
get on the ice much these days.

Chief Pish was a real character. He was one of the best bosses
I've ever had. He retired in the '90s and stayed incredibly active
in his church and the local community. When I jumped into the
flooded wash to save Mr. Roberts, Chief Pish wrote a fantastic
letter to our local newspaper supporting me. He was always so
proud of the department and the men and women that worked
with him. He really loved doing sit-ups and push-ups, even into
his eighties. I always thought he would live forever, his zest for

life was so fervent. I couldn't believe it when I heard the news that he died after a fall down his stairs at his house. After all those fires over the years, a stupid loss of balance did him in.

Wild Bill was the deputy fire marshal under Chief Pish. He was another fantastic person to work for. He was also a city council member and mayor of a neighboring city. He was beloved by a large portion of the residents and donated a lot of his time to making his city a better place to live and work. He knew all the top politicians in California. He was never boastful about his accomplishments and always remembered everyone's name. Bill was a fantastic family man, doting over his grandkids every chance he got.

He bought my old orange Corvette from me. I loved that car, and was only going to sell it to someone I liked and that would take good care of it. Bill helped me out with a few stories for the book and was so excited to read it. We would laugh so hard, and he would tell me a story I had never heard of about a few old-time chiefs, but then he would say, "You know, Reaper, maybe it's best if we don't add that one until the next book!" In an unreal turn of events, he died after complications from surgery last year. His passing really hit me hard.

Chief Larry Doan was a true leader. He kept our Station One "C" shift wild bunch in line—we would run through walls of fire for him. He was another amazing family man and was admired by everyone on the department. When I had my bar and restaurant, and later my skydiving center, I would always try to stay calm and think: "What would Chief Doan do in this situation?"

Chief Doan was also the quiet assassin when it came to fooling our crew with his own practical jokes. A group of us used to go out for happy hours on the weekends, including his daughter, Debbie. One afternoon the chief called Pike Pole into his office. He asked Pike Pole if he was going to marry his daughter, as they had also been hanging out with all of us. Pike Pole was confused as to what the hell the chief was talking about.

"Well, Pike Pole, I just want to know, now that you have gotten her pregnant, what the plan is?"

Pike Pole started sweating bullets, as nothing had happened with Debbie. And then it dawned on him: Chief Doan was just messing with him and loved watching him squirm! If there was a definition of what a battalion chief should be, it was for sure this guy. Larry was battling some health issues when he retired after over thirty years of service, but it seemed he was going to be OK. Sadly, he passed away not long after he retired. His death was a huge kick in the gut to those of us that worked with him. He was a true fire department legend.

Pike Pole, my Station One long-time partner in crime, is retired and enjoying traveling. The calls and antics with him really hold a special place with me. He was a great paramedic and firefighter and would make the shifts fly by with fun. We had some great off duty escapades as well. When I recently spoke with him, he reminded me of some classic stories that are better off left for maybe volume three or four! He's probably the only firefighter in history to retire after thirty-one years— just as skinny as his first day on the job! And yes, you guessed it, dude eats like a horse!

The Champ retired years ago and is enjoying life. I haven't seen him for quite a few years.

Bobby T and Norm, my old truck company compadres, are still enjoying their retirements.

The Geez was old when I worked with him in the 80s, that's why we called him that! Well, he was only in his late fifties, but he loved the nickname. The Geez became ill in his eighties. I went to the hospital to visit him right before he died. He was looking pretty frail, but lit up when he saw me.

"Reaper, how the hell are you!" And then he laughed and wondered if all the nearly dead folks in the hospital heard him yell Reaper! We had a good laugh over that. We spoke for a few hours about the old days at Station One, his family, and my family and what he was planning to do when he got out of the hospital. I knew he wasn't leaving there and knew it was the last time I would see him. I think deep down, he knew too. He told me I needed to bring a cold beer for him if I visited again. He died a few weeks later.

The Viking is living the good life, retired and hitting golf balls every day with his wife in Utah. When I drive up to Montana every year to skydive, I stop in and say hi. He's probably the strongest firefighter I've ever known and is still in great shape for an old fart! I sure miss arguing with him at the firehouse kitchen table just to keep ourselves amused. I now call him the Mayor of Old Town, as he lives in an over fifty-five golf community. Everyone knows him, so a trip to the clubhouse after a round of golf is like being with a celebrity.

Horrible retired as a deputy chief of operations. Like me, he has teenagers and will get to spend a lot of time with his family now. I went on a *lot* of fires with him when we were on Truck One together, and we had a lot of fun off duty over the years, even if we did almost drown. Hopefully, he will bring the family down soon for a visit and some surfing and fishing. We'll be sure to check the weather and swells before heading out on a boat!

The Party Bob retired a couple years ago. He's another guy we must have trained the right way back in the old Station One days because he also made his way up to be a deputy chief. He's enjoying his family and teenage son and is living the good life at the beach. He has really been a great friend over the years. Bob and his wife are gracious hosts and have been so good to my visiting family and friends over the years. He's another guy spending a lot of time on the golf course these days, working on his game to keep up with the Viking.

Joey retired years ago and is living the good life with his wife on a Tennessee lake. I think he goes fishing every day. Our old Station Three crew gets together in Las Vegas once in a while. It's always so much fun to see him. Joey should have given classes on how to be a fire captain. He was fantastic to work with.

With Hop (in the middle) and Joey at a retirement
dinner a few years ago

The Bhagwan is enjoying retirement and traveling around. I haven't seen the him in a long time.

Wayne retired a couple years ago. He's enjoying retirement and is always ready with a funny story and loves to laugh. He's part of the old Station Three crew, and when we get together, it gets loud! I want to thank him for writing a hilarious story for this book. Another victim of a Chief Doan prank!

Hose Clamp Eddie retired years ago and is enjoying traveling with his wife and enjoying his grandkids. He was another great example of what a battalion chief should be.

Rob G Rob was another of our Station One "C" shift alumni that made it big. He held nearly every rank on the department and made it all the way to *the* fire chief. He had the political savvy to move up the ranks, as he never really took a side during heated firehouse debates on whatever the kitchen table topic of the day was. The Viking called him the Fence Sitter years ago.

Rob was great to work with; we all knew he was one of those firefighters that was going to do well moving through the ranks. We had a lot of fun on- and off-duty adventures. Rob started looking rather ill right before he retired. No one really knew what was going on with his health. I about dropped the phone when Jethro Bodine called to tell me Rob G Rob passed away at the way, way too young age of fifty-five, just a few months after retiring.

The Angel Falls crew: Steve is back in London and has hung up his parachute. He still enjoys traveling. We have lost track of Adrian over the years. Tragically, Duane, who was one of the best humans I've ever met, died a few years after our trip on a wing suit jump in Switzerland.

Mark, my El Cap partner, is still skydiving and helps with my boogies once in a while.

Randy, my old roommate, is doing great. We've been friends forever! We still get together when we can. He has helped me with my skydiving events and with the opening of my drop zone in Oceanside. We have been through a lot together over the years. A person couldn't ask for a better friend.

With Doak, on the left, and Randy at sushi a few years ago

461

Chuck is still going strong in his old age and can still hold his breath underwater longer than anyone I know. I always try to stop in and visit him when I get back to the area. And, I never, ever, let him forget about not having any cooking fuel for the lobsters!

Doak is doing fantastic. He spends a lot of time SCUBA diving and traveling with his wife. We drove up to Montana together last year. It's a twenty-four-hour drive from Southern California, but with him next to me, it seems like twenty-four minutes! He's truly one of the best people I know, and I wonder how I got so lucky to have people like him in my life. We have had a *lot* of adventures together. A true wingman for the ages.

Gerry O', and the rest of the players from the LA Blazers early days, are all doing well. Spence still enjoys his smokes and martinis, but has hung up the goalie pads years ago. Some of the players can't skate these days due to bad hips, knees, and backs. We aren't getting any younger! Big John is still playing in his seventies. He was at the Burbank rink playing with Alan Thicke, and helped work on him, the day he dropped on the ice and later died.

Hop is truly my brother from another mother. We were partners at Station Three for about six years. My car is parked at his house, and when I get back from Costa Rica for visits, it's giant hugs from Hop and his wife—then the laughing starts! His two sons are grown, so I've my own room at their house. We talk often, and tell each other "I love you, brother" at the end of every call.

Hop is a fire-department legend. Working with him was a treat, and he's another firefighter that made the twenty-four-hour shifts fly by. We've spent nearly every Kentucky Derby together for the past thirty-two years. We always go to an off-track facility or casino and scream and yell for our picks! The pandemic ruined our plans this year, but we listened to the race together over the phone. Zoom? Nope, we're both too "Fred Flintstone" for that level of technology! He had a flip phone until just last year. When we're together, it's always never long enough.

I finally got Hop to jump out of an airplane. Here he is with my former chief instructor and San Diego City fire engineer, Nick. I think they were having fun!

Jethro Bodine is without a doubt one of the funniest, most loving and true characters I've ever met. He's retired and living the good life in Utah, not too far from the Viking. His four kids are now grown, which makes me feel really old. I stop in to also visit with them when I head to Montana each summer. I spent years working with him, and one of the only things I miss about the job is steering behind him in the tiller truck. We talk often, and he helped me with a few of the stories. We also tell each other "I love you" at the end of each phone call. He was a hell of a firefighter; we have probably been to a few thousand calls together. I could probably write another book titled *The Tales of Jethro*: he has so many stories.

Me with Bodine (in the middle) and the Viking a few years ago at Bodine's house. The room behind us has a lot of memorabilia from our fire service days.

My dad was an only kid, and my mom's brothers and sisters have all passed away, except for her youngest sister, my Aunt Pegge, who's still going strong at almost eighty-nine years young. I'm sure I'll hear from her about my use of swear words in the book soon!

Right before I retired in 2010, Kristine used her amazing legal skills and found my birth mother, Kathy. It wasn't easy, as I was born in Pennsylvania and adopted in Ohio. Thankfully, Kristine navigated the ridiculous red tape. Kathy and I have a fantastic relationship, and I've an entire family I'm getting to know. Her sister, Linda, is on the Fire Police in Pennsylvania. The fire service, I guess it's in my blood!

Kathy is truly the strongest woman I've ever known.

Two amazing women that I love dearly: Aunt Pegge on the left and my mom Kathy on the right during a visit last summer.

Three decades of running into burning buildings went by in a flash (no pun intended!)! I really hope this book has made you smile.

I'm signing off from the hammock now.

Life is good, hug your friends.

THE WASH RESCUE

I wasn't going to add this story in the book; however, my wife insisted I did, so I've saved it for last.

On February 6, 1998, I was working on Truck Seven with the engineer Jethro Bodine, my firefighter partner Manny, and a captain. It was raining for days and this shift saw no end in sight to the downpour. I asked Manny if we had our flotation devices and other swift water rescue equipment. We had some rope bags to throw to a victim, but no life vests or throw rings. The chief in charge of swift water training hadn't trained all the shifts on rescue techniques, so rescue equipment was locked up at the training center.

We ran a couple of emergency calls into downtown and stopped at our favorite burrito stand on the way back for our lunch. The alarm came in just as we finished eating.

"Engine Seven, Truck Seven, Engine Six, swift water rescue, victim is in the wash, last seen heading towards Hellman Avenue."

We ran to the rigs and headed in the direction of the wash, looking to get downstream of the victim at one of the bridges that crossed over the giant V-shaped cement wash. On the way, I made a safety harness around my legs and waist out of webbing and hooked in a metal carabiner. We pulled up to a bridge that was a few miles downstream of where the victim was last seen and looked up river. The victim was coming, bobbing up and down, and his head dipping under the water repeatedly! He was about a half mile up stream. Manny and I grabbed a rescue rope and he held it while I hooked it into my carabiner with a few quick wraps and I slid down over the bridge railing onto the water's edge. There was a firefighter from the neighboring department there already tied in to try and grab the victim.

Our captain was yelling at me from the bridge to grab the victim and not to let him go!

As he came bobbing by us, the firefighter missed him. I managed to get a hand on his coat, but it was so slippery from the water, I lost the grip. I jumped into the wash to grab him and my rope came untied.

That was it. I was now in the wash in only a pair of sneakers, gym shorts and a sweat shirt, so I swam to catch up to the victim. I knew that the wash opened up to a giant open area that formed a lake at the end during the rainy season. There were a lot of trees at the end to grab on to so we didn't end up in the Pacific Ocean.

I caught up to the drowning man and asked if he knew how to swim. He was gagging on swallowed gulps of runoff water and said he couldn't swim. He showed me his feet: his shoes were worn off and his feet were bleeding from going so many miles down the wash. We were in about four to five feet of chilly, muddy water.

He begged me to not let him drown.

I wrapped my hands tightly around his hood on his jacket and held his head above water. We were slowly heading down to the next bridge and I was hoping a bunch of firefighters from our city and the neighboring department would be there, as we had now floated into their jurisdiction.

His name was Terry. I filled him in on what was about to happen and what we needed to do to survive this ordeal together. There would be a bunch of people throwing ropes at us and we need to catch them, keeping them away from wrapping our necks. We would swing to shore and they would pull us out. If we missed the ropes and went into the big lake, we had to swim to the trees and hang on until they could come get us.

He begged louder not to let him drown, coughing as the waste water flew out of his mouth.

It was weird. One of my biggest fears was always drowning in fast moving water. I would never, ever go river rafting, instead opting for the calmness of SCUBA diving. But I had this sense of calm about me that everything was going to be fine, and I told Terry it wasn't our day to go. We kept on drifting downstream with the raindrops pelting us in total quiet.

I started running through some options.: The sides were steep and we probably couldn't get out. And I really didn't want to risk hitting my head on the cement side and rolling back into the wash unconscious. I managed to maneuver us left and right in the current a little bit. That was good info in case we needed to get closer to a rescue rope.

As we came around a bend in the wash, there it was, the calvary had arrived! There were a bunch of fire department vehicles and people scrambling on the bridge. I let Terry know this was showtime and to grab a rope if he could. We started speeding up as the wash goes downhill a little bit before the bridge, and there's a huge drain on the upstream side of the bridge that was spitting out thousands of gallons of water into the wash. We had to go right by it to clear the bridge. This was going to get dicey!

As we passed by the drain outlet we flew up in the water and then went under for a brief second. We came up under the bridge and when we just cleared it, in like a rocket came a rescue rope! Bodine raced like the wind in the ladder truck and had beaten everyone to the next bridge when I went in the drink. Manny, my partner that day, was a tremendous baseball player with a rocket arm. He threw a dart with the rescue rope bag right over my right shoulder. I grabbed the line as it slit open the palm of my hand with all of the friction and wrapped it tightly around my wrist, still hanging on to Terry with my left hand. When we got the rope extended there was a hell of a jerk, snapping my shoulder muscles. I managed to hang on and swing to shore. A group of firefighters hauled us up out of the water.

The entire rescue was filmed by a local cameraman that would go on all types of emergency calls and sell his footage to the local television news stations. He caught the entire last part on video.

I was fine, but I had to go to the hospital to get checked out under Battalion Chief Hose Clamp Eddie's orders. Bodine blew his knee out running down to the water's edge, twisting his leg in some rocks.

As you can imagine, it was quite the kerfuffle between the departments, and everyone wondering how I ended up with no safety gear in the water. Hose Clamp Eddie was the battalion chief that day and he was very calm about everything that was going on. He took our captain aside and settled him down a bit.

The hospital emergency room was packed with reporters wanting the story and an interview. The video of the rescue went all across the Los Angeles news, CNN and Fox News, and internationally. Rob G Rob was now a captain and they brought him in to be the public information officer. He kept the reporters at bay before I came out to give a brief statement. Big Fred, the chief of the department, stopped in to the ER. He was on his way to a retirement dinner for our longtime dispatch center supervisor. He was happy I wasn't too worse for wear and thanked me for saving the man's life. He said it was pretty ballsy but to never do that again.

I called my parents when I got back to the firehouse. The video was going to go national and I didn't want them to worry. It ended up being shown on Oprah's show and NBC Dateline interviewed me for an episode at the firehouse. It made the nightly national news in the USA and Canada for almost a week straight. I received thank you letters and phone calls from complete strangers around the world—that really blew me away. I still have the letters, tucked away in an envelope with all of my notes for this book. And of course, all of my fire department friends from around North America and others rang my phone off the hook.

I went "viral" before going viral was a thing, I guess!

On one hand, I saved a person from certain death. On the other hand, we should have never been there without the proper safety gear. During the investigation and critique of the call, Big Fred constantly had my back. He was old school fire service and knew we did what we had to do to save a citizen.

And he was good with that.

Later that year at our annual awards luncheon, with many of the citizens I took an oath to protect, my parents, fellow firefighters, and my LA Blazer teammates in attendance, I was the first firefighter in our fire department's history to receive the highest award for bravery, the Cross of Valor.

Chief Big Fred presenting me with the Medal of Valor

With my Blazer teammates, left to right, Doak, Will, Gerry O', Jeremy,
Justin, being photo bombed by Rupe

Horrible was awarded a "Life Saving" medal for a trench collapse
rescue and Hop was awarded one for the "Christine the Truck"
incident. Both were my firefighter partners over the years
and are top-notch humans.

What a career . . .

ABOUT THE AUTHOR

Rich Grimm spent over thirty-three years in the fire service. Starting as a volunteer firefighter in his sleepy Ohio hometown, he became a full-time firefighter in a neighboring city in Pennsylvania at the age of nineteen. After four years, he migrated to California, spending twenty-six years on a suburban fire department near Los Angeles.

Enjoy this book of his tales, written from his hammock on a beach in Costa Rica, where he now resides with his wife, daughter, three dogs and three cats, and an endless amount of monkeys as neighbors

He kept notes during those years and has written about all of the unique, funny, and endless firehouse pranks he either witnessed or was involved in.